The Besterman World Bibliographies

The Besterman World Bibliographies

Academic Writings

A BIBLIOGRAPHY OF
BIBLIOGRAPHIES

By Theodore Besterman

TOTOWA, N. J.
Rowman and Littlefield

1971

Published by
Rowman and Littlefield
A Division of
Littlefield, Adams & Co.
81 Adams Drive
Totowa, N. J. 07512

★

Copyright © 1939, 1947, 1965, 1971
by Theodore Besterman
Printed in the United States of America

★

Typography by George Hornby
and Theodore Besterman

ISBN 0-87471-044-8

Contents

Academic Writings   1

Special Subjects   127

Preface

I have explained in the Introduction to the successive editions of *A World bibliography of bibliographies* why I decided to arrange it alphabetically by specific subjects. Since that decision was taken, and after prolonged experience of the book in use, I have had no reason to regret it, nor among the many letters I have received from librarians has there been a single one complaining of the alphabetical form of the *World bibliography*.

The *World bibliography of bibliographies* covers all subjects and all languages, and is intended to serve reference and research purposes of the most specific and specialised kind. Yet contained in it are broad and detailed surveys which, if relevant entries throughout the volumes are added to them, can serve also the widest reference inquiries, and be useful to those who seek primary signposts to information in varied fields of inquiry.

Therefore I can only thank Rowman and Littlefield for having gathered together all the titles in some of the major fields found throughout the 6664 columns of the fourth edition (1965-1966) of *A World bibliography of bibliographies*.

Preface

These fields are:

1. Bibliography
2. Printing
3. Periodical Publications
4. Academic Writings
5. Art and Architecture
6. Music and Drama
7. Education
8. Agriculture
9. Medicine
10. Law
11. English and American Literature
12. Technology
13. Physical Sciences
14. Biological Sciences
15. Family History
16. Commerce, Manufactures, Labour
17. History
18. Geography

Of course these categories by no means exhaust the 117,000 separately collated volumes set out in the *World bibliography*, and the above titles will be added to if librarians wish for it.

Th. B.

Notes on the Arrangement

An Alternative to critical annotation

Consider what it is we look for in a normal bibliography of a special subject. Reflection will show, I think, that we look, above all, for completeness, just as we do in a bibliography of bibliographies. We desire completeness even more than accuracy (painfully uncongenial though it is for me to make such a statement); for in most cases a bibliography is intended to give us particulars of publications to which we wish to refer; thus we can always judge for ourselves (waiving gross errors) whether the bibliographer has correctly described these publications. On the other hand, anything that is omitted is lost until rediscovered.

The question is, therefore, whether it is possible to give some indication of the degree of completeness of a bibliography without indulging in the annotation which is impossible in a work of the present scope and scale. It seemed to me that this could be achieved, to a considerable extent, by recording the approximate number of entries set out in it. This method is, of course, a rough-and-ready one, but experience shows that it is remarkably effective: and I hope that its novelty will not tell against it.

The recording of the number of works set out in a bibliography has another advantage in the case of serial publications: it displays in statistical form the development of the subject from year to year—often in a highly significant manner.

This procedure, then, is that which I have adopted, the number of items in each bibliography being shown in square brackets at the end of the entry. This, I may add, is by no means an easy or mechanical task, as can be judged from the fact that this process, on the average, just about doubles the time taken in entering each bibliography.

Supplementary information in footnotes

I have said that this method of indicating the number of entries is intended to replace critical treatment; but it is not possible to exclude annotation altogether, for a certain minimum of added information is indispensable. Consequently many of my entries will be seen to have footnotes, in which the following types of information are recorded: a few words of explanation where the title is inaccurate, misleading, obscure, or in-

Notes

sufficiently informative; a statement to that effect where a work is in progress, where intermediate volumes in a series have not been published, or where no more have been published; an attempt to clarify complicated series; a note that a book was privately printed or in a limited number of copies, where this does not exceed 500, or in some abnormal manner, as on one side of the leaf, on coloured paper, or in a reproduction of handwriting, or with erratic pagination; when I have come across copies containing manuscript or other added matter, I have recorded the fact; substantial corrections and additions to bibliographies are sometimes published in periodicals, and I have noted a good many of these—but without aiming at anything even remotely approaching completeness, the attainment of which would be impossible. Various minor types of information are also occasionally to be found in the footnotes.

Owing to the great increase in the number of bibliographies reproduced directly from typewritten copy, such publications are designated by an asterisk at the end of the entry; this device saves a good deal of space.

Place of publication

The place of publication is not shown when it is London in the case of an english book and

Notes

Paris in the case of a french one. In the case of a series or sequence of entries, however, the absence of a place of publication means that it is the same as the place last shown in the series. The same applies to the names of editors and compilers. The place of publication is given as it appears on the titlepage, but prepositions are omitted even if violence is done to grammatical construction.

The Order of entries

Under each heading the order of the entries is chronological by date of publication; in the case of works in successive volumes or editions the chronological order applies to the first volume or edition. In suitable long headings an additional chronological order by period covered has been created; see, for instance, France: History, or Drama: Great Britain.

Method of collating

An effort has been made, so far as space allows, to give detailed and accurate information of the kind more usually found in small bibliographies. For instance, I have paid special attention to the collation of bibliographies in several (or even numerous) parts or volumes. It is, in fact, difficult to understand why it is usually considered necessary to give collations of works in a single volume, where difficulties seldom occur (from the point of view of systematic bibliography), but not of a work in several volumes, where confusion much more frequently arises. An occasional gap in the collations of such publications will be noticed. This is because, naturally enough, I have not been able in every case to see perfect sets; and I have thought it better to leave a very small number of such blanks rather than to hold up the bibliography indefinitely.

Serial publications

Where successive issues of a serial publication are set out, the year or period shown is usually that covered by the relevant issue; in such cases no date of publication is given unless publication was abnormal or erratic in relation to the period covered.

Bibliographies in more than one edition

Where a bibliography has gone into more than one edition I have tried (though I have not always been able) to record at least the first and latest editions. Intermediate editions have also been recorded wherever it seemed useful to do so, that is, for bibliographies first published before 1800, and for those of special interest or importance; but in general intermediate editions, though examined, have not been recorded.

Notes

Transcription of titles

Titles have been set out in the shortest possible form consistent with intelligibility and an adequate indication of the scope of the bibliography; omissions have of course been indicated. The author's name, generally speaking, is given as it appears on the titlepage, amplified and interpreted within square brackets where necessary.

Anonymous bibliographies

Far too large a proportion of bibliographical work is published anonymously. This is due, in part, to the all too common practice of library committees and similar bodies of suppressing altogether or of hiding in prefaces the names of those who have compiled bibliographies and catalogues for them. I have spent a good deal of time in excavating such and other evidences of authorship, and the result may be seen in the large number of titles preceded by names enclosed within square brackets.

Th. B.

Academic writings.

[under this heading are entered bibliographies of theses, university publications and similar academic writings; for publications on universities and similar bodies see Education; bibliographies of publications by or about specific universities &c. are here entered only in section 3, and elsewhere under the names of the universities.]

1. Periodicals, 5.
2. General, 5.
3. Subjects.
   Advertising, 11.
   Africa, 12.
   Agriculture, 12.
   America, 13.
   American Indians, 14.
   American literature, 14.
   Anatomy, 15.
   Anthropology, 15.
   Art, 15.
   Asia, 16.
   Banking, 16.
   Belgium, 17.

Academic Writings

Bible, 17.
Biology, 17.
Canada, 18.
Chemistry, 18.
Classical studies, 19.
Czechoslovakia, 20.
Disciples of Christ, 20.
Distribution, 20.
Domestic science, 20.
Drama, 21.
Economics, 21.
Education, 22.
Electricity, 31.
Engineering, 32.
English studies, 32.
Finance, 33.
Fish, 33.
Fluid mechanics, 33.
Folklore, 33.
Forestry, 34.
Games, 34.
Geology, 34.
Geophysics, 35.
Germany, german studies, 35.
History, 35.
Hygiene, 36.
India, 37.

2

Academic Writings

Japan, 37.
Journalism, 37.
Labour, 37.
Law, 38.
Librarianship, 42.
Mathematics, 42.
Medicine, 43.
Music, 48.
Natural history, 48.
Netherlands, 49.
Obstetrics, 49.
Ophthalmology, 49.
Pacific, 50.
Pharmaceutics, 50
Philology, 51.
Philosophy, 52.
Physical training, 52.
Physics, 52.
Political science, 53.
Psychology, 53.
Radio, 54.
Reading, 54.
Roman catholic church, 54.
Romance languages and literatures, 54.
Russia, 55.
Saar, 55.
Scandinavia, 55.

Science, 55.

Sociology, 57.

Sweden, 57.

Technology, 57.

Theology, 58.

Trade, 60.

United States, 60.

Veterinary science, *see* Medicine.

Water, 62.

William Wordsworth, 62.

4. Countries.

Africa, south, 63.

Argentina, 65.

Australia, 65.

Austria, 65.

Belgium, 66.

Canada, 67.

Cuba, 67.

Denmark, 68.

Finland, 68.

France, 68.

Germany, 76.

Great Britain, 91.

India, 93.

Italy, 93.

Netherlands, 94.

Poland, 96.

4

Russia, 97.

Scotland, 99.

Spain, 99.

Sweden and Finland, 100.

Switzerland, 102.

United States.

   i. Periodicals, 104.

   ii. General, 105.

Uzbekistan, 126.

1. *Periodicals*

INTERNATIONAL guide to the student press. International union of students: [Prague 1956]. pp.34.

2. *General*

CASPAR THURMANN, Bibliotheca academica, de rebus et juribus non tantum academiarum, & academicorum, sed etiam doctorum, aliorumq; eruditorum, extra academias viventium. Halæ Magdeburgicæ 1700. pp.[xvi].264. [6000.]

CHRISTIAN MISLER, Catalogus universalis disputationum atque scriptorum in qualibet facultate, nempe theologica, juridica, medica & philosophica, quae in quamplurimis academiis & gymnasiis, aliisque locis celebrioribus, tam intra—quam extra Germaniam, per hoc semestre hybernale ann. 1699 & 1700. [-1703] . . . prodierunt. Lipsiæ

1700–1703.pp.[vi] 42+48+48+48+48+44+48. [2578.]

P. C. EHRT, Catalogus disputationum . . . a viris . . . in diversis academiis . . . habitarum. [Ehrfurt] 1727. pp.[ii].210. [4000.]

JOHANN JACOB LECHNER, Catalogus dissertationum cum veterum, tum recentiorum, varii argumenti, secundum literarum ordinem conscriptus. . . . Tomus primus. Norimbergæ 1826. pp.vi.86. [3000.]

A–Buder only; no more published; reissued in 1833 as 'opera P. W. Baeumleri'.

CATALOGUS dissertationum academicarum quibus nuper aucta est Bibliotheca bodleiana. Oxonii 1834. pp.[ii].448.[lxiii]. [30,000.]

CH. FR. WALTHER, Catalogue méthodique des dissertations ou thèses académiques imprimées par les Elzevir de 1616 à 1712, recueillies . . . dans la Bibliothèque impériale publique à Saint-Pétersbourg. Bruxelles 1864. pp.107. [1079.]

CATALOGUE des dissertations et écrits académiques provenant des échanges avec les universités étrangères et reçus par la Bibliothèque nationale.

[i]. 1882. 1884. pp.101. [1500.]

[ii]. 1883. 1884. pp.125. [2000.]
[iii]. 1884. 1885. pp.129. [2000.]
[iv]. 1885. 1886. pp.119. [2000.]
[v–vi]. 1886–1887. 1889. pp.[iii].351. [5000.]
[vii]. 1888. 1891. pp.110. [2500.]
[viii]. 1889. 1892. pp.124. [2500.]
[ix]. 1890. 1893. pp.120. [2500.]
[x]. 1891. 1893. pp.135. [2750.]
[xi]. 1892. 1894. pp.[iii].139. [2750.]
[xii]. 1893. 1895. pp.[iii].144. [2750.]
[xiii]. 1894. 1895. pp.[iii].135. [2750.]
[xiv]. 1895. 1896. pp.[iii].139. [2750.]
[xv]. 1896. 1897. pp.[iii].153. [3000.]
[xvi]. 1897. 1898. pp.163. [3250.]
[xvii]. 1898. 1899. pp.172. [3500.]
[xvii]. 1899. 1900. pp.163. [3250.]
[xix]. 1900. Rédigé par m. É[mile] Laloy.
    1901. pp.200. [3500.]
[xx]. 1901. 1902. pp.220. [4000.]
[xxi]. 1902. 1903. pp.255. [5000.]
[xxii]. 1903. 1904. pp.276. [5500.]
[xxiii]. 1904. 1905. pp.295. [6000.]
[xxiv]. 1905. 1906. pp.283. [5500.]
[xxv]. 1906. 1907. pp.291. [6000.]
[xxvi]. 1907. 1908. pp.323. [6500.]
[xxvii]. 1908. 1909. pp.347. [7000.]
[xxviii]. 1909. 1910. pp.[iii].coll.736. [6000.]

xxix.1910. 1911. pp.[iii].coll.806. [6500.]

xxx. 1911. 1912. pp.[iii].coll.824. [6500.]

xxxi. 1912. 1913. pp.[iii].coll.830. [6500.]

xxxii. 1913. 1916. pp.[iii].coll.798. [6500.]

xxxiii–xxxvii. 1914–1918 [–1920]. 1919–1922. pp.94+95–250. [4500.]

xxxviii.1919.

xxxix. 1920.

xl. 1921. Rédigé par É. Laloy et [Jean Charles] Roman d'Amat. 1923. pp.[iii]. coll.78. [700.]

xli. 1922. 1924. pp.[iii].coll.262. [2000.]

xlii–xliii. 1923–1924. 1925. pp.[iii].coll.152. [1250.]

no more published.

ACADEMIES. British museum: Catalogue of printed books: 1885–1886. coll.1018.100, [12,500]

BIBLIOGRAPHISCHER monatsbericht über neu erschienene schul- und universitätsschriften. Herausgegeben von der Zentralstelle für dissertationen und programme von [*afterwards:* der Buchhandlung] Gustav Fock. Leipzig.

i. 1889–1890. pp.[iii].186. [3500.]

ii. 1890–1891. pp.[iii].144. [3345.]

iii. 1891–1892. pp.[iii].152. [3629.]

iv. 1892–1893. pp.[iii].160+34. [3630.]

Academic Writings

v. 1893–1894. pp.[iii].152+36. [3688.]
vi. 1894–1895. pp.[ii].157+40. [3690.]
vii. 1895–1896. pp.[ii].161+43. [3720.]
viii. 1896–1897. pp.[ii].177+45. [3974.]
ix. 1897–1898. pp.[ii].157+44. [3476.]
x. 1898–1899. pp.[ii].169+54. [3744.]
xi.1899–1900. pp.[iii].156+47. [3529.]
xii. 1900–1901. pp.[ii].162.11+46. [3729.]
xiii. 1901–1902. pp.[ii].162+37. [3756.]
xiv. 1902–1903. pp.[iii].202+41. [5151.]
xv. 1903–1904, pp.[ii].209+45. [4967.]
xvi. 1904–1905. pp.[iii].204.16+65. [4934.]
xvii. 1905–1906. pp.[iii].176+64. [4532.]
xviii. 1906–1907. pp.[iii].211+67. [4491.]
xix. 1907–1908. pp.[iii].199.22+72. [5097.]
xx. 1908–1909. pp.[ii].81.240. [6161.]
xxi. 1909–1910. pp.[ii].56.220. [5240.]
xxii. 1910–1911. pp.[iii].229.20+70. [6560.]
xxiii. 1911–1912. pp.[ii].191+40. [4995.]
xxiv. 1912–1913. pp.[ii].261.78. [7139.]
xxv. 1913–1914. pp.[ii].247.72. [6674.]
xxvi. 1914–1915. pp.[iv].244.71. [6556.]
xxvii. 1915–1916. pp.[iii].144.41. [3873.]
xxviii. 1916–1917. pp.[iii].156.36. [3086.]
xxix. 1917–1918. pp.[iii].122.28. [2317.]
xxx. 1918–1919. pp.[iii].56. [1382.]
xxxi. 1919–1920. pp.[iii].136.4.48.28. [4110.]

9

xxxii. 1920–1921. pp.[iii].68.7.24. [1937.]
xxxiii. 1921–1922. pp.[iii].44.14.4. [1186.]
xxxiv. [1922–1923]. pp.xxxi.xxxii.xxxii.
   [635.]*
xxxv. [1923–1924]. pp.54. [903.]*
— [index to vols.xxxiv–xxxv.]pp.[iii].41.83.
xxxvi. 1925. pp.[iii].88.36. [2475.]
xxxvii. 1926. pp.[iii].16.16.16.16.32.41.
   [2783.]
xxxviii. 1927. pp.[iii].142.16.41. [4152.]
xxxix. 1928. pp.[iii].171.67. [4834.]
xl. 1929. pp.[iii].82.204. [6026.]
xli. 1930. pp.[iii].93.240. [7246.]
xlii. 1931. pp.[iii].16.216. [6526.]
xliii. 1932. pp.[iii].86.216. [6658.]
xliv. 1933–1934. pp.[iii].89.224. [7030.]
xlv. 1934–1935. pp.[iii].95.248. [7754.]
xlvi. 1935–1936. pp.[iii].112.288. [8989.]
xlvii. 1936–1937. pp.[iii].113.320. [10,250.]
xlviii. 1937–1938. pp.[iii].106.312. [9891.]
xlix. 1938–1939. pp.[iii].107.312. [9868.]
l. 1939–1940. pp.[iii].290.100. [9230.]
li. 1940–1941. pp.[iii].248.84.

the second pagination from vol.iv consists of a subject index.

[CELESTINO SCHIAPARELLI], Elenco delle accademie, società, istituti scientifici, direzioni di periodici ecc. che ricevono le pubblicazioni della R. accademia dei Lincei. Roma 1903. pp.182. [3000.]

—— [second edition. By Giuseppe Gabrieli]. 1908. pp.iii–viii.421. [4000.]

WANT list of publications of educational institutions. Library of Congress: Washington 1909. pp.14. [275.]

WILHELM FALCKENHEINER, Universitäts-matrikeln. Göttingische nebenstunden (no.6): Göttingen 1928. pp.[iv].25. [250.]

HERMANN MUNDT [vol. ii: ELISABETH DENKSCHERZ], Biobibliographisches verzeichnis von universitäts- u. hochschuldrucken (dissertationen) vom anfang des 16. bis ende des 19. jahrhunderts. [1934-] 1936–1939. pp.[ii].720+240. [26,845.]
A–Plouquet only; no more published.

CATALOG of the programmschriften collection, the university of Pennsylvania library [Philadelphia]. Boston 1961. pp.[v].117.260. [5454.]*

3. Subjects

Advertising

WILLIAM A[HLERS] NIELANDER, A selected and

annotated bibliography of literature on [bibliography of] public relations. University of Texas: Bureau of business research: Bibliography series (no.3): Austin 1948. pp.14. [200.]*

— — [fourth edition]. 1961. pp.[v].58. [400.]*

Africa

JOCHEN KÖHLER, Deutsche dissertationen über Afrika. Ein verzeichnis für die jahre 1918–1959. Deutsche Afrika-gesellschaft: Bonn 1962. pp. [249]. [795.]*

A LIST of american doctoral dissertations on Africa. Library of Congress: General reference and bibliography division: Washington 1962. pp.[v]. 69. [700.]

Agriculture

CHRONOLOGICAL list of departmental publications. University of Reading: Agricultural economics department: 1937 [&c.].
details of this work are entered under Agriculture: Agricultural economics, below.

HANDLIST of publications, 1924–1945. University college of Wales: Department of agricultural economics: Aberystwyth 1945. pp.[iv].33. [350.]*

BIBLIOGRAPHIE der landwirtschaftlichen hochschulschriften . . . in deutscher sprache . . . auf dem gebiet der land- und forstwirtschaftswissenschaften. Deutsche bücherei: Sonderbibliographien (no.1 &c.): Leipzig.

1945–1952. [Edited by] Werner Dux, Curt Fleischhack. . . . (no.1). pp.xii.172. [1992.]
1953–1956. . . . (no.14). pp.xii.339. [3452.]

ANGELA HERNÁNDEZ-ARANGO and LUCÍA VALENCIA M., Tesis de grado presentadas a la Facultad nacional de agronomía de Medellín. Medellín 1954. ff.[i].27. [246.]*

HOCHSCHULARBEITEN aus agrarökonomik und agrarsoziologie. Bibliographie abgeschlossener und laufender dissertationen. Forschungsgesellschaft für agrarpolitik und agrarsoziologie (no.63 &c.): Bonn.*

[i]. 1945–1957. Bearbeitet von Th[eo] Dams. . . . (no.63): 1957. pp.173. [1541.]
[*continued as:*]
Forschungsarbeiten aus agrarökonomik und ländlicher soziologie.

ii. 1957–1960. Bearbeitet von Joachim Lunze. . . . (no.144): 1962. pp.145. [723.]
in progress.

America

THESES on pan american topics prepared by

candidates for degrees in universities and colleges in the United States. Pan american union: Columbus memorial library: Bibliographic series (no.5): Washington 1931. pp.52. [502.]*

— Third edition. 1941. ff.[i].4.170. [1671.]*

HARRY KANTOR, A bibliography of unpublished doctoral disserations [*sic*] and masters theses dealing with the governments, politics and international relations of latin America. Inter-american bibliographical and library association (1st ser., vol.xiii): Gainesville, Fla. 1953. pp.85.

SURVEY of research investigations in progress and contemplated in the field of latin american subjects in colleges and universities in the United States and Canada. Gainesville 1953 &c.

in progress; details of this work are entered under America, below.

American Indians

FREDERICK J. DOCKSTADER, The american Indian in graduate studies. A bibliography of theses and dissertations. Museum of the american Indian: Contributions (vol.xv): New York 1957. pp.xvii. 399. [3684.]

American literature

CLYDE H[ULL] CANTRELL and WALTON R. PATRICK,

Academic Writings

Southern literary culture. A bibliography of masters' and doctors' theses. [University, Ala. 1955]. pp.xiv.124. [2529.]*

JAMES [LESLIE] WOODRESS, Dissertations in american literature, 1891–1955. Durham, N.C. 1957. pp.x.100. [3000.]
—— 1891–1961. 1962. pp.xii.138. [3500.]

Anatomy

CHRISTIAN LUDWIG SCHWEICKHARD, Tentamen catalogi rationalis dissertationum ad anatomiam et physiologiam spectantium ab anno MDXXXIX. ad nostra usque tempora. Tubingae 1798. pp.vi.444. [3328.]

Anthropology

JOHN ALAN JONES, List of unpublished doctoral dissertations and masters theses in the field of anthropology bearing on north american Indians north of Mexico. Department of justice: Washington [1952]. ff.19. [225.]*

Art

PRISCILLA HISS and ROBERTA FANSLER, Research in fine arts in the colleges & universities of the United States. Carnegie corporation: New York 1934. pp.vii.224. [215.]

Academic Writings

BIBLIOGRAPHIE des handwerks. Verzeichnis der dissertationen. Universität Göttingen: Seminar für handwerkswesen: Göttingen.*

    1933–1944. Bearbeitet von Marianne Kidery. 1956. ff.147. [953.]

    1945–1952. Bearbeitet von Gerhard Kämpf. 1955. ff.[48]. [300.]

VINCENT LANIER, Doctoral research in art education. [Los Angeles] 1962. pp.[ii].52.[xx]. [450.]*

Asia

CURTIS W. STUCKI, American doctoral dissertations on Asia, 1933–1962, including appendix of master's theses at Cornell university. Cornell university: Southeast Asia program: Data paper (no.50): Ithaca, N.Y. 1963. pp.204.

Banking

CUMULATIVE catalogue of theses, 1937–1940. American bankers association: Graduate school of banking: New York [1940]. pp.[ii].65. [225.]

    —— 1937–1942. pp.97. [200.]

CUMULATIVE catalogue of theses 1937–1956. American bankers association: Graduate school of banking: New York [1957]. pp.199.

Academic Writings

Belgium

J[ULIETTE] L. DARGENT, Bibliographie des thèses et mémoires géographiques belges, 1904-1953. Commission belge de bibliographie: Bibliographia belgica (no.3): Bruxelles 1953. pp.35. [181.]
— — 2ᵐᵉ édition. 1904–1958. . . . (no.42): 1959. pp.xi.85. [347.]*

Bible

JAC. FRID. [JOHANN FRIEDRICH] WILDESHAUSEN, Bibliotheca disputationum theologico-philologicarum in V. & N. testamentum. Hamburgi 1702. pp.[viii].112. [2000.]
— — Editio prior rectior. Lipsiæ 1710. pp.[xx]. 326. [4500.]

CHRISTOPH HEINRICH SCHETELIG, Bibliotheca disputationum theologico-philologico-exegeticarum in V. & N. testamentum. Hamburgi 1736–1737. pp.[vi].374+[iv].312. [15,000.]
this is actually a new edition of the work entered next above.

MARTIN J. BUSS, Old testament dissertations 1928–1958. [Ann Arbor 1959]. pp.x.57.

Biology

OTTO E. A. HJELT, Sveriges biologiska disputa-

17

tions- och program-litteratur. 1700–vårterminen 1910. Bidrag til kännedom af Finlands natur och folk (vol.lxx, no.1): Helsingfors 1911. pp.viii.210. [2250.]

Canada

UNIVERSITY dissertations, theses and essays on canadian geography. Department of mines and technical surveys: Geographical branch: Bibliographical series (no.3): Ottawa 1950. ff.[i].8. [100.]*

— Addenda no.1. 1951. ff.[i].3. [40.]*

RESEARCH on immigrant adjustment and ethnic groups. A bibliography of unpublished theses 1920–1953. Canadian citizenship branch: Ottawa 1955. pp.[ii].ii.131. [650.]*

Chemistry

HENRY CARRINGTON BOLTON, A select bibliography of chemistry, 1492–1897.... Section VIII. Academic dissertations. Smithsonian institution: Miscellaneous collections (no.1253): Washington 1901. pp.iv.534. [7500.]

TITLES of theses submitted for doctoral degrees in chemistry and chemical engineering at american educational institutions October 1, 1951 to October 30, 1952. American chemical society:

Committee on professional training: Washington [1953]. pp.[iv].55. [600.]

FACULTIES, publications, and doctoral theses in chemistry and chemical engineering at United States universities. American chemical society: Committee on professional training: [Washington].*

    1953. pp.[ii].vi.245. [10,000.]
    1954.
    1955. pp.v.440. [16,000.]
            [*continued as:*]
Directory of graduate research.

HANS BERNDT and SIEGFRIED GÜNTHER, Bibliographie der deutschen hochschulschriften zur chemie. Ein systematisches verzeichnis der in den jahren 1957–1958 an deutschen universitäten und hochschulen eingereichten dissertationen und habilitationsschriften. Deutsche bücherei: Sonderbibliographien (no.23): Leipzig 1960.pp.viii.264. [2631.

Classical studies

GUSTAV FOCK, Catalogus dissertationum philologicarum classicarum. Leipzig. pp.[iv].224.148. 72.124. [18,300.]
   —— Editio II. 1910. pp.[iii].652.[27,500.]

Academic Writings

Czechoslovakia

DISSERTATIONEN zur problematik des böhmisch-mährischen raumes. Sudetendeutsches archiv: Schriftenreihe (no.1): München.*
   i. [1955]. ff.[i].iv.42. [182.]
   ii. 1956. ff.[i].iv.47. [261.]

Disciples of Christ

CLAUDE E[LBERT] SPENCER, Theses concerning the Disciples of Christ, the churches of Christ, and the Christian church. Disciples of Christ historical society: Canton, Mo. 1941. ff.[iii].55. [175.]*

Distribution

BIBLIOGRAPHY of graduate theses in the field of marketing written at U.S. colleges and universities 1950–1957. New York university: Graduate school of business administration: [New York 1957]. ff.[ii].92. [1400.]*

Domestic science

TITLES of completed research from home economics departments in american colleges and universities, 1918 to 1923. Bureau of education: Home economics circular (no.18): Washington [1924]. pp.14. [250.]

Academic Writings

ELIZABETH WIEGAND, Selected bibliography of theses and research in family economics, home management and related areas. American home economics association: Washington 1954. pp.16. [225.]*

—— Supplement . . . by Emma G. Holmes. 1957. pp.19. [250.]*

Drama

SAMUEL SELDEN, *ed.* Research in drama and the theatre in the universities and colleges of the United States, 1937–1942. A bibliography. American educational theatre association: Meadville, Pa. [1944]. pp.[iv].48. [750.]

GISELA SCHWANBECK, Bibliographie der deutschsprachigen hochschulschriften zur theaterwissenschaft von 1885 bis 1952. Gesellschaft für theatergeschichte: Schriften (vol.58): Berlin 1956. pp. xiv.566. [3309.]*

HANS JÜRGEN ROJEK, Bibliographie der deutschsprachigen hochschulschriften zur theaterwissenschaft von 1953 bis 1960. Gesellschaft für theatergeschichte: Schriften (vol.61): Berlin 1962. pp. xvi.170. [558.]*

Economics

DIE WIRTSCHAFTSWISSENSCHAFTLICHEN hoch-

schularbeiten. Institut für angewandte wirt-
schaftswissenschaft: Berlin [1936]. pp.vii.310.
[2500.]

INDEX of publications of bureaus of business
and economic research. Associated university
bureaus of business and economic research:
[Eugene, Or.] 1950 &c.

*in progress; details of this work are entered under
Economics, below.*

TESIS doctorales de la Facultad de ciencias
económicas, 1916–1951. Catálogo. Universidad
nacional: Buenos Aires 1952. pp.83. [543.]

G[IRIRAJ] P[RASAD] GUPTA, Economic investigations in India. (A bibliography of researches in
commerce and economics approved by indian
universities). Agra [1961]. pp.[iii].v.81. [750.]

STELLA TRAWEEK, A survey of university business and economic research reports . . . 1957
through 1961. Small business administration:
Washington [1961]. pp.xii.642. [2298.]*

[—] — [another edition]. A survey . . . 1957
through 1963. Prepared by Cynthia R. Bettinger,
Charles T. Clark. 1963. pp.xiii.690. [3623.]*

Education

TITLES of masters' and doctors' theses in education accepted by colleges and universities in the United States. University of Illinois: Bureau of educational research: [Urbana].*

    1917–1919. Compiled by Walter S[cott] Monroe. ff.vii.65. [871.]
    1919–1920. ff.[v].47. [467.]
        [continued as:]
Masters' and doctors' [&c.].
    1920–1922. ff.[iv].46. [476.]
    1922–1923. ff.[vi].73. [961.]
        [continued as:]
Titles of masters' [&c.]
    1923–1925. ff.vii.119. [1688.]
    1925–1927. ff.xi.252. [3509.]
no more published.

REGISTER of Teachers college doctors of philosophy, 1899–1928[–1934], Columbia university: New York 1928–1934.

HERBERT A[RTHUR] TONNE, Index of dissertations of the School of education, New York university. New York 1930. [630.]
    — — [second edition]. 1932. pp.48. [1070.]

RUSSEL T[AAFFE] GREGG and THOMAS T[RISTAM] HAMILTON, Annotated bibliography of graduate theses in education at the university of Illinois.

[University of Illinois:] College of education: Bureau of educational research: Bulletin (no.55): Urbana 1931. pp.80. [252.]

ABSTRACTS of dissertations and theses in education at the university of Michigan. Bureau of educational reference and research: Ann Arbor.
- i. 1917–1931. [By Warren R. Good.] pp.vi. 137. [70.]
- ii. 1931–1932. pp.[vi].130. [110.]

[CHARLES HUBBARD JUDD], Annotated list of graduate theses and dissertations, the Department of education, the university of Chicago, 1900–1931. Chicago [1932]. pp.[vi].119. [1235.]*

RECENT theses in education ... deposited with the Office of education and available for loan. Office of education: Pamphlet (no.26): Washington 1932. pp.iii.41. [242.]
— [another edition]. Doctors' theses [&c.]. By Ruth A. Gray.... (no.60): 1935. pp.[ii].69. [797.]

FREDERICK EBY and S. E. FROST, Graduate theses and dissertations in the field of education at Baylor university, Southern methodist university, Texan christian university, Texan technological college, the university of Texas, West Texas state teachers college. [Austin 1934]. pp.85. [823.]

Academic Writings

[CHESTER ARTHUR BUCKNER], Annotations of theses and dissertations in education, university of Pittsburgh, School of education. Phi delta kappa: XI chapter: Pittsburgh 1934. pp.[viii].56. [588.]

—— [third edition]. Directory of holders of graduate degrees in education, with titles of theses and dissertations, university of Pittsburgh, School of education. [By John Alfred Vietz]. 1945. pp.90. [1065.]

FREDERICK J. WEERSING, ed. Annotated index of theses and dissertations. University of Southern California: School of education: Alpha epsilon chapter of Phi delta kappa: [Los Angeles] 1936. pp.[vi].133. [1782.]

TITLES of graduate theses and dissertations, the Department of education, the university of Chicago, 1932–1935 [&c.]. Chicago 1936 &c.*

SUMMARIES of doctoral dissertations and masters' theses accepted during 1936, Teachers college, university of Nebraska. University of Nebraska: Extension division: Educational monographs (no.10 = University of Nebraska publication, no.121): Lincoln 1937. pp.40. [42.]

REGISTER of doctoral dissertations accepted in

partial fulfillment of the requirements for the degree of doctor of philosophy. Columbia university: Teachers college: New York.

> i. 1899–1936. Edited by Anvor Barstad, Ruth Moses and Eleanor M[ontgomery] Witmer. 1937. [1072.]

NOUVART TASHJIAN, *ed.* List of doctors' and masters' theses in education, New York university, 1890–June 1936. New York 1937. pp.[ii].ii–iii. 117. [1565.]*

ABSTRACTS of theses for the degree of master of science in education, 1923–1929. College of the city of New York: School of education: New York 1939. pp.118. [381.]

SUMMARIES of masters' theses in school administration, Teachers college, university of Nebraska, 1925–1940. University of Nebraska: Extension division: Educational monographs (no.15 = University of Nebraska publication, no.136): Lincoln [1940]. pp.94. [320.]

ABSTRACTS of masters' and doctors' theses in education, the university of Texas, Austin 1940 &c.

in progress.

ABSTRACTS of dissertations. George Peabody

college for teachers: Nashville, Tenn.1942 &c. *in progress.*

A[NNIE] M[ARGARET] BLACKWELL, A list of re-searches in education and educational psychology presented for higher degrees in the universities of the United Kingdom, Northern Ireland, and the Irish Republic from 1918 to 1948. National foundation for educational research in England and Wales: [1950]. pp.173. [2250.]

—— A second list . . . 1949, 1950, and 1951. 1952. pp.127. [1000.]

—— Supplement for . . . 1952 and 1953. [1954]. pp.62. [600.]

STUDIES in education. Abstracts of theses. Indiana university: School of education: Bloomington.

    [i]. 1945–1949. pp.108. [17.]
              [continued as:]
Thesis abstract series. Studies in education.

    ii. 1950. pp.138. [21.]
    iii. 1951. pp.195. [30.]
    iv. 1952. pp.325. [53.]
    v. 1953. pp.258. [44.]
    vi. 1954. pp.242. [40.]
    vii. 1955. pp.379. [60.]
    viii. 1956. pp.378. [50.]*

MASTER's theses in education. Cedar Falls, Iowa. 1951 &c.
in progress; details of this work are entered under Education, below.

GRADUATE theses in education 1913–1952. Partial list. Canadian education association: Toronto [1952]. pp.[ii].34. [500.]*
— Supplement A. 1954. ff.10. [125.]*

BIBLIOGRAPHY of studies completed at Utah colleges and universities. Utah educational research bulletin (vol.4, no.1 &c.): [Salt Lake City] 1952 &c.
in progress; details of this work are entered under Academic writings: United States.

MARY LOUISE LYDA and STANLEY B[ARBER] BROWN, Research studies in education. A subject index of doctoral dissertations, reports, and field studies. Boulder, Colo. 1953 &c.*
in progress.

THESES in education and educational psychology accepted for degrees at australian universities; supplement, 1951–1953. Australian council for educational research: Library: Melbourne 1955. ff.[iv]. 34. [205.]*

WALTER CROSBY EELLS, American doctoral dissertations on education in countries of the middle east. Middle east institute: Washington 1955. ff.28. [200.]*

w[ILLIAM] w[ESTON] CARPENTER and A[RLIE] G[LENN] CAPPS, Areas of educational administration considered in doctoral dissertations, university of Missouri. University of Missouri: Bulletin (vol.58, no.27): [Columbia 1957. pp.51. [360.]

GRADUATE research in education, West Virginia university, 1898–1959. Morgantown 1959. pp.[iii]. 139. [977.]*

WILLIAM R. SHUNK and FRANKLIN PARKER, History of education, philosophy of education and comparative education: annotated bibliography of doctoral dissertations at the university of Texas 1923–1958. University of Texas: Department of history and philosophy of education: [Austin] 1959. ff.[66]. [81.]*

FRANKLIN PARKER, Negro education in the U.S.A.; a bibliography of doctoral dissertations. Austin 1960. ff.9. [100.]*

THESES and dissertations, Department of education, Louisiana state university, 1917–1960. [Baton Rouge] 1961. ff.[ii].44. [550.]*

Academic Writings

FRANKLIN PARKER, Canadian education; bibliography of doctoral dissertations. Austin [1961]. ff.9. [131.]*

FRANKLIN PARKER, Jewish education: a partial list of american doctoral dissertations. Austin 1961. ff.5. [60.]*

FRANKLIN PARKER, The community junior college. . .; a bibliography of . . . doctoral research dissertations. Austin [1961]. pp.16. [188.]*
— — [supplement]. [1961]. pp.4. [38.]

FRANKLIN PARKER. The american high school; a bibliography of . . . doctoral dissertations. Austin [1961]. ff.9. [131.]*

FRANKLIN PARKER, Audio-visual education; a bibliography of doctoral dissertations. Austin [1961]. ff.17. [209.]*

FRANKLIN PARKER, Teacher education; a bibliography of . . . doctoral dissertations. Austin [1961]. pp.32. [705.]*

FRANKLIN PARKER, Catholic education: a partial list of american doctoral dissertations. Austin 1961. ff.12. [189.]*

FRANKLIN PARKER, School desegregation; a list of doctoral dissertations. [Austin 1961]. pp.[8]. [94.]*

30

Academic Writings

FRANKLIN PARKER, Biographies of educators; a partial list of american doctoral dissertations. Austin [1961]. pp.8. [120.]*

FRANKLIN PARKER, Fifty years of the junior high school; ... a bibliography of ... doctoral dissertations. Austin [1961]. pp.15. [131.]*

LAWRENCE C[ALVIN] LITTLE, A bibliography of doctoral dissertations on adults and adult education. University of Pittsburgh: Department of religious education: Pittsburgh 1962. pp.[iii].82. [1000.]*

—— Revised edition. 1963. pp.iv.163. [2500.]*

FRANKLIN PARKER, Latin american education research. An annotated bibliography of ... United States doctoral dissertation. University of Texas: Institute of latin american studies: Austin [1963]. pp.63. [269.]*

Electricity

KATHARINE MAYNARD and MURRAY F[RANK] GARDNER, A classified list of theses in electrical engineering presented at Massachusetts institute of technology, 1902–1929, including also recent research reports. Massachusetts institute of technology: Publication [vol.lxv, no.46 = Department of electrical engineering, no.65:] Cambridge 1929. pp.108. [1280.]

Academic Writings

Engineering

R[OY] A[NDREW] SEATON, *ed*. Engineering experiment station record. . . . A summary of engineering research at the land-grant colleges and universities. Association of land-grant colleges and universities: [Lancaster, Pa. 1929]. pp.vii.98.

[—] — [another edition]. [Edited by John Hard Lampe]. [1945]. pp.134. [3500.]

RALPH R[EGINALD] MCNAY, A subject list of theses in civil and sanitary engineering . . . 1913–1938. Massachusetts institute of technology: Library: Cambridge 1939. ff.68. [1650.]*

English studies

VERZEICHNIS der an der universität Leipzig erschienenen dissertationen und fakultätsschriften auf englischem gebiet. [Leipzig 1900]. pp.7. [150.] *covers works published during the period 1875–1900.*

RICHARD MUMMENDEY, Die sprache und literatur der Angelsachsen im spiegel der deutschen universitätsschriften, 1885–1950. Eine bibliographie. [Bonner beiträge zur bibliotheks- und bücherkunde (vol.1)]: Bonn 1954. pp.xvi.200. [2989.]

RICHARD D[ANIEL] ALTICK and WILLIAM R. MATTHEWS, Guide to doctoral dissertations in victorian

Academic Writings

literature 1886–1958. Urbana 1960. pp.vii.119.
[2105.]

Finance

VLADISLAV ADOLFOVICH RAKHLEVSKY and GEOR-
GY IVANOVICH USHAKOV, Диссертации по
финансам, денежному обращению, кредиту,
бухгалтерскому учету и анализу хозяйст-
венной деятельности, защищенные на уче-
ную степень доктора и кандидата экономи-
ческих наук с 1939 по 1961 г. Библиографический указатель. Москва 1962. pp.112.
[1500.]

Fish

ROBER M. JENKINS, *ed.* Bibliography of theses on
fishery biology ... and related subjects. Sport fishing institute: [Washington] 1959. pp.[iii]80.
[1743.]*

Fluid mechanics

J[OE] W[ILLIAM] JOHNSON, Theses and reports
on fluid mechanics and related fields (1900–1945)
and publications of Fluid mechanics laboratory
(1926–1945). University of California: Department of engineering: Berkeley 1945. ff.[i].35.
[343.]*

Folklore

LUTZ RÖHRICH, Bibliographie volkskundlicher

dissertationen an deutschen universitäten, 1945–1950. Stuttgart 1951. pp.18. [214.]

Forestry

THESES submitted for advanced degrees in the subject matter of forestry, in colleges and universities of the United States. Oregon state college library: [Corvallis] 1938. ff.[i].86. [840.]*

KATHERINE W[HIPPLE] HUGUES, RAY A. YODER and WILLIAM I. WEST, Forestry theses accepted by colleges and universities in the United States 1900–1952. Oregon state college: Bibliographic series (no.3): Corvallis 1953. pp.140. [2638.]

Games

BETTY [MARGARET ELIZABETH] VAN DER SMISSEN, A bibliography of research theses and dissertations only related to recreation. State university of Iowa: Iowa City 1962. pp.[ii].ii.119. [961.]*

Geology

[DANIEL S. TURNER], Bibliography of geology theses, colleges and universities of the United States. Denver [1954]. pp.[iii].483. [5750.]*

[—] — [another edition]. Bibliography of theses written for advanced degrees in geology and related

34

sciences at universities and colleges in the United States and Canada through 1957. By [Byron] John Chronic and Halka Chronic. 1958. pp.[428]. [11,091.]*

Geophysics

GEORGE E. TARBOX, Bibliography of graduate theses on geophysics in U. S. and canadian institutions. Colorado school of mines: Quarterly (vol.53, no.1): Golden 1958. pp.vi.55. [450.]*

Germany, german studies

HOCHSCHULSCHRIFTEN zur neueren deutschen geschichte. Eine bibliographie. Kommission für geschichte des parlamentarismus und der politischen parteien: Bonn.

    i. 1945–1955. Von Alfred Milatz und Thilo Vogelsang. pp.3–142. [2325.]

F. NORMAN, *ed.* Theses in germanic studies . . . (excluding english), approved for higher degrees in the university of Great Britain and Ireland between 1903 and 1961. University of London: Institute of germanic languages and literatures: 1962. pp.viii.46. [455.]

History

PH[ILIPP] A[LEXANDER] F[ERDINAND] WALTHER,

Systematisches repertorium über die schriften sämtlicher historischer gesellschaften Deutschlands. Darmstadt 1845. pp.xxx.649. [7000.]

BULLETIN of the Institute of historical research. Theses supplement. 1933 &c.
in progress; details of this work are entered under History, below.

[CHARLES CUMBERLAND], Classified list of master of arts dissertations in history, 1895–1940 inclusive. University of Texas: [Austin 1941]. ff.[i]. iii.63. [985.]*

LIST of doctoral dissertations in history now in progress at universities in the United States. American historical association: Washington [1949]. pp.55. [1634.]
500 copies printed.

Hygiene

T[HOMAS] K[IRK] CURETON, Doctorate theses reported by graduate departments of health, physical education and recreation, 1930–1946, inclusively. [Washington 1949]. pp.[39]. [420.]
limited to United States theses.

THOMAS K[IRK] CURETON, Masters theses in health, physical education and recreation.

Academic Writings

American association for health, physical education and recreation: Washington 1952. pp.iii. 292. [3878.]*

India

KLAUS LUDWIG JANERT, Verzeichnis indienkundlicher hochschulschriften. Deutschland, Österreich, Schweiz. Wiesbaden 1961. pp.ix.80. [931.]

Japan

DOCTORAL dissertations on Japan, accepted by american universities, 1912–1939. Japan institute: New York 1940. ff.vii.17. [89.]*

Journalism

FR[ITZ] FRANZMEYER, Presse-dissertationen an deutschen hochschulen 1885–1938. Herausgegeben von Walther Heide. Börsenverein der deutschen buchhändler: Leipzig 1940. pp.167. [1353.]

Labour

INDUSTRIAL relations theses and dissertations submitted at seventeen [thirty-eight] universities. University of California: Institute of industrial relations: Berkeley.*

  1949–1950. Edited by Gwendolyn Lloyd. ff.[i].40. [350.]

  1950–1951.

37

1951–1952.

1952–1953.

1953–1954. Edited by G. Lloyd and Paul M.
Miles. ff.[i].vii.67. [600.]

1954–1955. ff.[i].vii.40. [473.]

1955–1956. ff.[i].ix.47. [529.]

NED ROSEN and RALPH E[DWARD] MCCOY, Doctoral dissertations in labor and industrial relations
1933–1953. University of Illinois: Institute of labor
and industrial relations: Bibliographic contributions (no.5): Champaign 1955. ff.iv.86. [1031.]*

DISSERTATIONS and theses relating to personnel
administration accepted by american colleges and
universities. Civil service commission: Library:
Washington.*

1955. pp.20. [200.]

1956. pp.[ii].23. [250.]

[EMILE POULAT], Soixante-dix ans d'études asso-
ciationnistes. Les thèses universitaires françaises,
1885–1955. Archives internationales de sociologie
de la coopération (1957, no.1): Aubenas [printed]
1957. pp.176–204+183–216. [383.]

Law

CARL JOHANN FOGEL, Antiqua et nova bibliotheca disputationum dnn. hamburgensium lite-

Academic Writings

ratorum juridica. Hamburgi 1730. pp.94. [800.]

JUDAS THADDÄUS ZAUNER, Biographische nachrichten von den salzburgischen rechtslehrern von
der stiftung der universität an bis auf gegenwärtige zeiten. Salzburg 1789. pp.[xvi].144. [500.]

CHRISTOPH WEIDLICH, Volständiges verzeichniss aller auf der Königl. preussl. Friedrichsuni-
versität zu Halle . . . herausgekommenen juristischen disputationen und programmen. Halle
1789. pp.xii.151.74. [1500.]

CHRISTIAN LUDWIG SCRWEICKHARD [sic,
SCHWEICKHARD], Tentamen catalogi rationalis
dissertationum ad medicinam forensem et poli-
tiam medicam spectantium ab anno MDLXIX ad
nostra usque tempora. Francofurti a.M. 1796.
pp.[ii].viii.156. [616.]

[GOTTFRIED LEBRECHT GŒTHE AND CARL GOTT-
LOB RICHTER], Lexicon literaturae academico-
iuridicas, quo tituli dissertationum, programma
tum aliarumque commentationum iuridicarum
ab academiarum initiis usque ad finem anni 1835
editarum. Lipsiae 1836–1838. pp.xiii.394+[ii].
548. [20,000.]

[COUNT] A[DOLPHE CHARLES THÉODORE] DE

FONTAINE DE RESBECQ, Notice sur le doctorat en droit, avec . . . une analyse chronologique des lois, statuts, décrets . . . relatifs à cet enseignement, de 1791 à 1857, suivie . . . du catalogue raisonné des thèses soutenues de 1851 à 1857. 1857. pp.[iii]. lxiii.199. [500.]

CH[ARLES] LE FORT, Catalogue des thèses soutenues devant la faculté de droit de Genève de 1821 à 1877. Genève 1878. pp.32. [208.]

CATALOGUE d'une collection de thèses publiées dans les Pays-Bas donnée à la Bibliothèque nationale par le Service des échanges internationaux. I. Droit. 1884. pp.69. [750.]

T[OBIAS] M[ICHAEL] C[AREL] ASSER, De academische rechtsliteratuur van Amsterdam, 1787–1887. Amsterdam 1887. pp.viii.32. [600.]
—— 1e vervolg, 1887–1892. 1893. pp.[ii].23. [93.]

THÈSES de droit soutenues aux universités des Pays-Bas 1700–1898 [*on cover:* Catalogus dissertationum juridicarum defensarum in academiis Neerlandiae 1700–1898]. Leyde 1898. pp.[iv].151. [3878.]

G. ZIELER and TH. SCHEFFER, Das akademische

Deutschland. Biographisch-bibliographisches handbuch für die universitäten des Deutschen reiches, als ergänzung zum Deutschen universitätskalender. Band II. Die juristischen fakultäten. Leipzig 1905. pp.[ii].iv.86. [1500.]

RÉPERTOIRE des thèses de droit soutenues dans les facultés françaises. Période 1911–1920.
[i. 1910–1911]. pp.29.xvi. [650.]
ii. 1911–1912. pp.31–53.xvii–xxvii. [500.]
iii. 1912–1913. pp.[viii].55–76. [450.]
no more published.

[GUSTAVO OLIVERA and JUAN SCHREIBER], Catálogo de la colección de tesis jurídicas. Universidad nacional de la Plata: Buenos Aires 1914. pp.101. [1000.]

RÉPERTOIRE de thèses de droit comparé soutenues à la Faculté de droit de Paris pendant les années 1900 à 1930. Université de Paris: Faculté de droit: Bulletin de documentation législative et sociale (no.23): [1931]. pp.70. [1000.]

CATALOGUE des thèses de droit soutenues devant les facultés de France. Université de Paris: Faculté de droit: Bibliothèque.
i. 1933. pp.32. [429.]
ii. 1934. pp.3–39. [430.]

iii. 1935. pp.3–47. [466.]
iv. 1936. pp.3–54. [503.]
v.1937. pp.3–55. [521.]
no more published; includes legal theses sustained in other faculties.

CATÁLOGO de tesis de la Facultad de derecho. Universidad nacional mayor de San Marcos: [Lima] 1944. pp.149. [2800.]

L[UCIEN] CAES and R[OGER] HENRION, Collectio bibliographica operum ad ius romanum pertinentium. Series II. Theses. Bruxelles 1950 &c.

DIE VÖLKERRECHTLICHEN dissertationen an den westdeutschen universitäten 1945–1957. Deutsche gesellschaft für völkerrecht: Karlsruhe 1958. pp.52. [500.]

Librarianship

DOROTHY CHARLES, Dissertations, theses, and papers of the Graduate library school, university of Chicago, 1930–1945. A bibliography. [Chicago 1945]. ff.[ii].28.[iv]. [132.]*

Mathematics

HENRY C[LAY] BADGER, Mathematical theses of junior and senior classes, 1782–1839. Harvard university: Library: Bibliographical contributions (no.32): Cambridge 1888. pp.14. [406.]

VERZEICHNIS der seit 1850 an den deutschen universitäten erschienenen doktor-dissertationen und habilitationsschriften aus der reinen und angewandten mathematik. Deutsche mathematikvereinigung: München 1893. pp.[iii].35. [1500.]

E[UGÈNE PIERRE] ESTANAVE, Nomenclature des thèses de sciences mathématiques soutenues en France dans le courant du XIXe siècle devant les facultés des sciences de Paris et des départements. 1903. pp.viii.44. [292.]

Medicine

JOHANN CARL HEFFTER, Museum disputatorium physico-medicum tripartitum. Zittaviae Lvsatorum 1756–1764. pp.[xl].480.80.84+14.298+[ii].299–526.92.88. [18,498.]
   the first volume was reissued in 1763 as a so-called 'Editio nova'.

JOHANN FRIEDRICH BLUMENBACH, Synopsis systematica scriptorvm qvibvs inde ab inavgvratione Academiae Georgiae Avgvstae d. XVII Sept. MDCCXXXVII vsqve ad sollemnia istivs inavgvrationis semisaecvlaria MDCCLXXXVII. disciplinam svam avgere et ornare stvdvervnt professores medici gottingenses. Gottingae 1788. pp.36. [500.]

STATUTA solennia de doctoratus in medicina gradu in Academia edinburgena capessando, a facultate medica proposita, et in posterum, jubente senata academico, observanda. [Edinburgh c.1800]. pp.36.

SEBASTIAN JOHANN LUDWIG, Critisches repertorium der auf in- und ausländischen höhern lehranstalten vom jahre 1781 bis 1800 herausgekommenen probe- und einladungschriften aus dem gebiete der arzneygelehrtheit und naturkunde. Erste abteilung, enthaltend das verzeichniss der schriften von 1781 bis 1790. Herborn 1803. pp.xvi.412. [2794.]

P[IERRE] SUË, Tables chronologique et alphabétiques des thèses in-8° soutenues à l'École de médecine de Paris . . . depuis le 28 frimaire an VII jusques et compris le 6 floréal an XII. 1806. pp.vii. 80. [406.]

LIST of the graduates in medicine in the university of Edinburgh, from MDCCV. to MDCCCLXVI. Edinburgh 1867. pp.vi.187.73. [6000.]
theses are recorded only from 1726.

G. H. FRIEDRICH FRÄNKEL, Bibliotheca medicinae

Academic Writings

militaris et navalis. . . . 1. Inaugural-abhandlungen. Thesen. Programme. Glogau 1876. pp.[ii].iv.68. [1250.]

no more published.

ABRAHAM GRÜNFELD, Verzeichniss der von der medicinischen facultät zu Dorpat seit ihrer gründung veröffentlichten schriften. Keiserliche universität Dorpat: Pharmakologisches institut: Historische studien (vol.iii): Halle a.S. 1893. pp.135. [3000.]

G. ZIELER and TH. SCHEFFER, Das akademische Deutschland. Biographisch-bibliographisches handbuch für die universitäten des Deutschen reiches, als ergänzung zum Deutschen universitätskalender. Band III. Die medizinische fakultäten. Leipzig 1906. pp.317. [5000.]

NOÉ LEGRAND, La collection des thèses de l'ancienne faculté de médecine de Paris depuis 1539 et son catalogue inédit jusqu'en 1793. Bibliothèque historique de la 'France médicale' (vol.l): 1913. pp.216. [1500.]

the theses listed cover the period 1763-1793 only.

CATÁLOGO de la colección de tesis, 1827-1917. Universidad nacional: Facultad de ciencias médicas: Biblioteca: Buenos Aires 1918. pp.496. [3750.]

TABLES (la première des noms des auteurs et la seconde des matières) des thèses soutenues à la Faculté de médecine de Paris.

1920–1921. pp.83. [631.]
1922. pp.60. [457.]
1923. pp.55. [418.]
1924. pp.67. [553.]
1925. pp.67. [552.]
1926. pp.79. [662.]
1927. pp.71. [559.]
1928. pp.64. [493.]
1929. pp.68. [519.]
1930. pp.67. [513.]
1931. pp.72. [571.]
1932. pp.79. [640.]
1933. pp.80. [626.]
1934. pp.103. [830.]

1935. pp.111. [930.]
1936. pp.108. [871.]
1937. pp.108. [910.]
1938. pp.108. [809.]
1939. pp.167. [1510.]
1940. pp.96. [674.]
1941. pp.72. [414.]

1942. pp.68. [360.]
1943. pp.52. [376.]
1944. pp.75. [498.]
1945. pp.126. [951.]
1946. pp.126. [882.]
1947. pp.86. [851.]
1948. pp.96. [956.]
1949. pp.128. [1101.]
1950. pp.139. [1146.]
1951. pp.144. [1237.]
1952. pp.136. [1117.]
1953. pp.127. [1037.]
1954. pp.128. [1071.]
1955. pp.136. [1139.]
1956. pp.136. [1133.]
1957. pp.136. [1114.]
1958.
1959. pp.140. [1055.]
1960. pp.136. [1039.]
in progress.

A[NDRÉ] HAHN, Table des thèses soutenues devant la Faculté de médecine de Paris en 1939. 1940. pp.167. [2250.]

SUBJECTS of theses submitted by fellows in the Mayo foundation for medical education and research who obtained graduate degrees in the university of Minnesota from January, 1915, to July 1945. [Rochester 1945]. pp.55. [1100.]

V. N. TERNOVSKY, Библиография диссертаций Медицинского факултета Московского университета. Москва 1949. pp.64. [861.]
covers the period 1791–1922.

JAHRBUCH der dissertationen. Rheinische Friedrich-Wilhelms-universität Bonn: Medizinische fakultät: Bonn 1951 &c.
in progress; details of this work are entered under Bonn, below.

Music

HANS [THEODORE] DAVID [*and others*], A list of doctoral dissertations in musicology and allied fields. Music teachers national association [&c.]: Denton, Texas 1951. ff.[i].41. [325.]*
limited to the universities of the United States and Canada.

RICHARD SCHAAL, Verzeichnis deutschsprachiger musikwissenschaftlicher dissertationen, 1861–1960. Gesellschaft für musikforschung: Musikwissenschaftliche arbeiten (no.19): Kassel 1963. pp.167. [2819.]

Natural history

JOHANN CARL HEFFTER, Museum disputatorium

physico-medicum tripartitum. Zittaviae Lvsatorum 1756–1764. pp.[xl].480.80.84+14.298+
[ii].299–526.92.88. [18,498.]
the first volume was reissued in 1763 as a so-called
'Editio nova'.

SUZANNE LAVAUD, Catalogue des thèses de doctorat ès sciences naturelles soutenues à Paris de
1891 à 1954. Faculté de pharmacie: Bibliothèque:
Paris 1955. pp.257. [1181.]

Netherlands

[WILLEM NIKOLAUS DU RIEU], Register van
academische dissertatien en oratien betreffende de
geschiedenis des vaderlandes. Maatschappij der
nederlandsche letterkunde: Commissie van geschiedenis en oudheidkunde: Leiden 1866.
pp.[iii].iv.104. [1601.]
— — Supplement. 1882. pp.[viii].47. [800.]

Obstetrics

CHRISTIAN LUDWIG SCHWEICKHARD, Tentamen
catalogi rationalis dissertationum ad artem obste-
triciam spectantium ab anno MDXV. ad nostra
usque tempora. Francofurti a.M. 1795. pp.viii.
232. [1200.]

Ophthalmology

CHARLES THOMAS, Répertoire méthodique des

thèses françaises d'ophtalmologie soutenues de 1904 à 1937. Laboratoire des tubes Dulcis: Monte-carlo [1938]. pp.36. [1300.]

Pacific

RÉPERTOIRE des thèses de sciences sociales sur le Pacifique sud. Commission du Pacifique sud: Document technique (no.102): Nouméa 1957. pp.x.85. [100.]

Pharmaceutics

PAUL [MARIE JEAN] DORVEAUX, Catalogue des thèses soutenues devant l'École de pharmacie de Paris, 1815–1889. 1891. pp.viii.76. [500.]

PAUL [MARIE JEAN] DORVEAUX, Catalogue des thèses de pharmacie soutenues en province . . . (1803–1894), suivi d'un appendice du "Catalogue des thèses . . . de Paris". 1894. pp.117. [800.]

GABRIEL GARNIER and ODETTE BARTHÉLEMY, Catalogue des thèses soutenues devant la Faculté de pharmacie de Paris de 1895 à 1940. 1941. pp.96. [802.]

—— Deuxième édition . . . augmentée des thèses soutenues de 1941 à 1959, par Suzanen Lavaud. 1960. pp.210. [1164.]

MARIE MARCHAL, Catalogue des thèses soutenues

devant la faculté de pharmacie de Nancy de 1873
à 1943. Université de Nancy: Nancy 1944. pp.48.
[257.]

Philology

HERMANN VARNHAGEN, Systematisches verzeichniss der auf die neueren sprachen, hauptsächlich
die französische und englische, sowie die sprach-
wissenschaft überhaupt bezüglichen programm-
abhandlungen, dissertationen und habilitationsschriften. Leipzig 1877. pp.[iii].iv.xix.100. [1750.]
also issued as a supplement to Bernhard Schmitz,
Encyclopädie des philologischen studiums der
neueren sprachen, *Greifswald &c.* 1859–1877.
—— Zweite... auflage. Besorgt von Johannes
Martin. 1893. pp.xvi.296. [4000.]

[MAURICE BLOOMFIELD], Bibliographia hopkinsiensis, 1876-1891. Part 1. Philology. Johns
Hopkins university: Baltimore 1892. pp.[iii].52.
[1000.]

WILHELM SCHONACK, Ein jahrhundert berliner
philologischer dissertationen (1810–1910). Wolfenbüttel 1914. pp.x.232. [1500.]

R[AY] M[ARCH] MERRILL, American doctoral
dissertations in the romance field, 1876–1926.
Institut des études françaises: New York 1927.
pp.88. [500.]

A[LBERT] H[UGH] SMITH and A[RTHUR] T[HOMAS] HATTO, A list of english, scandinavian and german theses in the university of London. London mediæval studies: Monograph (no.2): 1939. pp.viii.40. [403.]

Philosophy

HANS FLASCHE and UTTA WAWRZINEK, Materialien zur begriffsgeschichte. Eine bibliographie deutscher hochschulschriften von 1900–1955. Archiv für begriffsgeschichte (vol.5): Bonn 1960. pp.xix.718. [9491.]

Physical training

URSULA WEIDIG, Bibliographie der dissertationen aus körperkultur, körpererziehung, sport und verwandten gebieten. In- und ausländische dissertationen in deutscher sprache sowie an deutschen universitäten verteidigte fremdsprachige dissertationen von 1648 bis 1959. Mit einem anhang: habilitationsschriften. Deutsche hochschule für körperkultur: Bibliothek: Sportbibliographien (no.6): Leipzig 1960. pp.128.

Physics

VERZEICHNIS der veröffentlichungen aus der Physikalisch-technischen reichsanstalt, 1887 bis 1900. Berlin 1901. pp.53. [500.]

Academic Writings

a supplement appears in the Reichsanstalt's Die bis-
herige tätigkeit (*Braunschweig 1904*).

EUGÈNE [PIERRE] ESTANAVE, Nomenclature des
mémoires de physique expérimentale et de physique mathématique présentés en France dans le
courant du XIXᵉ siècle devant les facultés des
sciences en vue du doctorat. 1903. pp.20. [350.]

M. LOIS MARCKWORTH, Dissertations in physics. An indexed bibliography of all doctoral
theses accepted by american universities, 1861–
1959. Stanford 1961. pp.xii.803. [8418.]*

Political science

GEORGE R. LANOUE, A bibliography of doctoral
dissertations undertaken in american and canadian
universities 1940–1962 on religion and politics.
National council of the churches of Christ in the
U.S.A.: [New York 1963]. pp.v.49.

Psychology

LOUIS N. WILSON, List of papers in the field of
religious psychology presented at Clark university. Clark university: Library: Publications
(vol.ii, no.8): Worcester, Mass. 1911. pp.9. [122.]

LAWRENCE C[ALVIN] LITTLE, Researches in per-
sonality, character and religious education. A

bibliography of american doctoral dissertations
1885 to 1959. [Pittsburgh] 1962. pp.iv.215. [6304.]★

Radio

KENNETH R. SPARKS, A bibliography of doctoral
dissertations in television and radio. Syracuse
university: School of journalism: Syracuse, N.Y.
[1962]. ff.[ii].32. [352.]★

Reading

LEO C. FAY, WELDON G. BRADTMUELLER and
EDWARD G. SUMMERS, Doctoral studies in reading,
1919 through 1960. Indiana university: School of
education: Bulletin (vol.40, no.4): [Bloomington]
1964. pp.vi.80.★

Roman catholic church

DISSERTATIONS in american church history
(1889–1932). Catholic university of America:
American church history seminar bulletins (no.1):
Washington 1933. pp.27. [184.]
privately printed.

Romance languages and literatures

[HANS FLASCHE], Die sprachen und literaturen
der Romanen im spiegel der deutschen universitätsschriften, 1885–1950. Bonner beiträge zur

bibliotheks- und bücherkunde (vol.iii): Bonn
1958. pp.xxii.299. [4688.]
*also issued by the Bibliographical society of the
university of Virginia under the title of* Romance
languages and literatures *(Charlottesville)*.

Russia

JESSE J[OHN] DOSSICK, Doctoral research on Russia and the Soviet Union. [New York] 1960.
pp.[vii.]248. [2000.]

Saar

WALTHER CARTELLIERI, Verzeichnis der Saar-
dissertationen. Berlin 1933. pp.24. [126.[

Scandinavia

FRITZ MEYEN, Die nordeuropäischen länder im
spiegel der deutschen universitätsschriften, 1885–
1957. Bonner beiträge zur bibliotheks- und
bücherkunde (vol.iv): Bonn 1958. pp.xxii.126.
[1099.]
also issued under the title of The north european
nations.

Science

[LOUIS] ATH[ÉNAÏS] MOURIER, Notice sur le
doctorat ès sciences, suivie du catalogue des
thèses admises par les facultés des sciences depuis
1810. 1856. pp.79. [300.]

ALBERT MAIRE, Catalogue des thèses de sciences soutenues en France de 1810 à 1892. pp.xi.224. [1000.]

—— Revue décennale des thèses présentées à la faculté des sciences de Paris en vue du grade de docteur ès sciences du 1ᵉʳ janvier 1891 au 31 décembre 1900, avec l'indication des périodiques contenant la plupart de ces mémoires. Par E[ugène Pierre] Estanave. Arcis-sur-Aube 1901. pp.115. [347.]

DOCTORATES conferred in the sciences by american universities. 1919 &c.

details of this work are entered under Science: United States, below.

CATALOGUS van proefschriften vervaardigd ter verkrijging van de graad van doctor in één der natuurwetenschappen aan universiteiten of hoogescholen in Nederland in de jaren 1900–1930. [s.l.1931]. pp.206.

[GULIO PROVENZAL], Prolusioni di argomento scientifico lette nelle università a negli istituti superiori d'Italia per la inaugurazione dell'anno scolastico dal 1860 al 1930. Consiglio nazionale delle richerche: Roma 1932. pp.viii.150. [800.]

BARTON BLEDSOE, Masters' theses in science,

Academic Writings

1952. Washington [1954]. pp.252. [5588.]

Sociology

THÈSES de sciences sociales. Catalogue analytique international de thèses inédites de doctorat, 1940–1950. Unesco: Paris 1952. pp.236. [3215.]

Sweden

CATALOGUS dissertationum, quæ ad illustrandas res svecicas faciunt. Holmiæ 1765. pp.214. [xlviii]. [3000.]

Technology

PAUL TROMMSDORFF, Verzeichniss der bis ende 1912 an den technischen hochschulen des Deutschen reiches erschienenen schriften. Berlin 1914. pp.x.184. [2972.]

ANNOTATED list of 800 graduate theses and dissertations in industrial-arts education and vocational-industrial education accepted by institutions of higher learning in the United States, 1892–1933. [Iowa state college: Ames 1933]. ff.[xii].89. [800.]*

WILLIAM L[UTHER] HUNTER, Theses pertaining to industrial arts education. Iowa state college, 1922–1935. [Ames 1935].ff.[iv].18. [106.]*

Theology

CAROL. GODOFR. GUIL. [KARL GOTTFRIED WILHELM] THEILE, Thesaurus literaturae theologicae academicae sive recensus dissertationum, programmatum aliarumque commentationum theologicarum . . . quae ab antiquissimus usque ad recentissima tempora editae in collectione Goethiana lipsiensi sunt venales. [Pars prior]. Lipsiae 1840. pp.xiv.284. [7000.]

J. E. VOLBEDING, Index dissertationum, programmatum et libellorum quibus singuli historiae N.t. et antiquitatum ecclesiasticarum loci illustrantur. Lipsiae 1849. pp.iv.176. [6000.]

J. C. VAN SLEE, Catalogus dissertationum et orationum theologicarum defensarum et habitarum ab a. 1650 ad 1850 in academiis Neerlandiae, Germaniae, Sueciae, collectarum a Fred. Muller. Amstelodami 1868. pp.[ii].673. [10,375.]

A[UGUSTE] BOUVIER, La faculté de théologie de Genève pendant le dix-neuvième siècle. Thèses-concours-étudiants. Documents pour servir à l'histoire de l'académie de Genève (vol.i): Genève 1878. pp.viii.96. [280.]

HENRI HEYER, Catalogue des thèses de théologie soutenues à l'académie de Genève pendant les

XVIᵉ, XVIIᵉ, et XVIIIᵉ siècles. Documents pour servir à l'histoire de l'académie de Genève (vol.v): Genève 1898. pp.cxi.168. [476.]

G. ZIELER and TH. SCHEFFER, Das akademische Deutschland. Biographisch-bibliographisches handbuch für die universitäten des Deutschen reiches, als ergänzung zum Deutschen universitätskalender. [1. Band. Die theologischen fakultäten]. Leipzig 1905. pp.viii.83. [1500.]

P. GLORIEUX, Répertoire des maîtres en théologie de Paris au XIIIᵉ siècle. [Etudes de philosophie médiévale (vols.xvii–xviii):] 1933–[1934]. pp.[iii].468+[iii].518. [3500.]

[ÉMILE POULAT], Thèses et mémoires présentés en France de 1940 à 1954 et touchant à la sociologie des religions. Centre national de la recherche scientifique: Archives de sociologie des religions: 1956. pp.13. [180.]

LAWRENCE C[ALVIN] LITTLE, Bibliography of doctoral dissertations in character and religious education. University of Pittsburgh: Department of religious education: Pittsburgh [1960]. pp. [iii].273. [5000.]*

FRANKLIN H[AYWARD] KNOWER, Bibliography of

communications dissertations in american schools
of theology. [*s. l.* 1961]. ff.45. [863.]*

GEORGE R. LaNOUE, A bibliography of doctoral
dissertations undertaken in american and canadian
universities 1940–1962 on religion and politics.
National council of the churches of Christ in the
U.S.A.: [New York 1963]. pp.v.49.

Trade

FERN L. WILSON, Wilson's index of publications
by university bureaus of business research. [Cleveland 1957]. pp.303. [2500.]*

—— Supplement. 1957. ff.118. [1000.]*

United States

[MARY LOUISE RUKA], The Wisconsin region. A
bibliography of theses in the social sciences and
humanities. [University of Wisconsin centennial
committee: Madison 1949]. ff.[ii].42.12 [*sic,* 14].
[750.]*

THE SOCIOLOGY of the south: a bibliography
and critique of unpublished doctoral dissertations
and master's theses written on aspects of the
south, 1938–1948. Fisk university: Social science
institute: Social science source documents (no.6:)
Nashville 1950. ff.[i].iii.376. [223.]*

Academic Writings

CLAUDE ELLIOTT, Theses on Texas history . . . produced in the departments of history of eighteen Texas graduate schools and thirty-three graduate schools outside of Texas, 1907–1952. Texas state historical association: Austin 1955. pp.xi.280. [652.]

JAMES TAYLOR DUNN, Master's theses and doctoral dissertations on New York history, 1870–1954. (Revised). [s.l.] 1955. pp.20. [400.]

MARY E[LIZABETH] MORRIS, Bibliography of theses on Oklahoma in the university of Oklahoma library. University of Oklahoma: Institute of community development: Norman 1956. ff.[i]ii.104. [1250.]*

HOMER E[DWARD] SOCOLOFSKY, Kansas history in graduate study. A bibliography of theses and dissertations. Kansas state university of agriculture and applied sciences: Manhattan 1959. pp.64. [942.]*

JOHN CHAVIS, A brief survey of theses in Michigan history. [Detroit 1959]. ff.ii.pp.20. [300.]*

Veterinary science see Medicine

Academic Writings

Water

EMILY C. LUMBARD, Engineering, economic, social and legal aspects of water. Theses presented for higher degrees, University of California . . . 1900–1957. University of California: Water resources center archives: Report (no.2): Berkeley 1958. pp.[ii].73. [439.]*

GERALD J. GIEFER and CYNTHIA BARNES, Bachelor of science theses on water resources engineering, university of California, Berkeley. University of California: Water resources center archives: Report (no.6): Berkeley 1959. pp.[iii].93. [598.]*

GERALD J. GIEFER, LOIS JUDD and CYNTHIA BARNES, Theses on water resources, Stanford university, California institute of technology and university of Southern California. University of California: Water resources center archives: Report (no.7): Berkeley 1959. pp.iv.81. [561.]*

William Wordsworth

ELTON F. HENLEY, A check list of masters' theses in the United States on William Wordsworth. University of Virginia: Bibliographical society: [Charlottesville 1962]. pp.ii.29.[xi]. [381.]*

4. *Countries*

[*universities &c. are entered only under their names; see the note at the beginning of this heading.*]

Africa, south

A[NTHONY] M[EREDITH] LEWIN ROBINSON, Catalogue of theses and dissertations accepted for degrees by the south african universities... 1918–1941. Cape Town 1943. ff.ix.155. [1757.]*

REGISTER van huidige navorsing in die humaniora aan die universiteite [en ander inrigtings]. [Pretoria.]*

    1946.

    1947.

    1948.

    1949.

    1950. ff.[iv].72. [500.]

    1951. ff.[iii].48. [350.]

    1952. ff.[iii].36. [250.]

            [*continued as:*]

Register van huidige navorsing in die humaniora in Suid-Afrika.

    1953. pp.[viii].81.[500.]

    1954. pp.[viii].82. [500.]

    1955. pp.[vi].77. [500.]

    1956. pp.[viii].72. [450.]

Academic Writings

1957. pp.[viii].75. [450.]
1958. pp.[vii].58. [350.]
1959. ff.[iv].52. [300.]
in progress.

REGISTER van die huidige wetenskaplike navorsing aan suid-afrikaanse universiteite. Wetenskaplike en nywerheidnavorsingsraad: Biblioteek-en inligtingsafdeling: Pretoria.

1951. ff.164. [388.]
1953. pp.vi.212. [397.]*
1955. pp.viii.341. [545.]*
1956. pp.vii.251. [534.]*
1957. pp.viii.198. [538.]
1958. pp.viii.235. [636.]
1959. pp.vii.113. [587.]
1960. pp.vii.129. [787.]
1961. pp.vi.112. [768.]
1962. pp.vi.149. [899.]
in progress; also issued in an english edition.

STEPHANUS I[MMELMAN] MALAN, Gesamentlike katalogus van proefskrifte en verhandelinge van die suid-afrikaanse universiteite . . . 1942–1958. Potchefstroom 1959. pp.216. [2500.]
——— Aanvulling.
i. 1959. pp.iv.30. [500.]
ii. 1960. pp.iv.33. [400.]

64

Academic Writings

Argentina

[GUSTAVO OLIVERA and JUAN SCHREIBER], Catálogo de la colección de tesis jurídicas. Universidad nacional de la Plata: Buenos Aires 1914. pp.101. [1000.]

CATÁLOGO de la colección de tesis, 1827–1917. Universidad nacional: Facultad de ciencias médicas: Biblioteca: Buenos Aires 1918. pp.496. [3750.]

Australia

THESES in education and educational psychology accepted for degrees at australian universities; supplement, 1951–1953. Australian council for educational research: Library: Melbourne 1955. ff.[iv].34. [205.]*

MARY J[ACQUELINE MESTON] MARSHALL, Union list of higher degree theses in australian university libraries. University of Tasmania: Library: Hobart 1959. pp.vii.237. [3333.]*
—— Supplement. 1959 &c.
in progress.

Austria, see also *Germany*

JOHANN GUTSCHER, Systematisch geordnetes verzeichnis des wissenschaftlichen inhaltes der

von den oesterreichischen gymnasien und real-
gymnasien in den jahren 1850–1867 veröffentlichten programme. 1. Theil. Programm des Kais.
kön. gymnasiums: Marburg 1868. pp.xxii.71.
[850.]

JOSEPH BITTNER, Systematisch geordnetes verzeichnis der programm-arbeiten österreichischer
mittelschulen. Teschen [Czernowitz] [1890–]
1891–1906.
covers the period 1874–1905.

WILHELM KRAUSE, Gesamtverzeichnis der programme und festschriften der schulen Österreichs,
1945–1955. Wien [1956]. pp.vii.310.

Belgium

J[ULIETTE] L. DARGENT, Bibliographie des thèses
et mémoires géographiques belges, 1904–1953.
Commission belge de bibliographie: Bibliographia belgica (no.3): Bruxelles 1953. pp.35. [181.]
— — 2ᵐᵉ édition. 1904–1958. . . . (no.42): 1959.
pp.xi.85. [347.]*

J[ULIETTE] L. DARGENT, Des institutions à carac-
tère universitaire ou scientifique et les publications
dont elles disposent. Commission belge de biblio-

graphie: Bibliographia belgica (no.23): Bruxelles
1958. pp.97. [500.]

Canada, see also *United States*

GRADUATE theses in education 1913-1952. Partial list. Canadian education association: Toronto
[1952]. pp.[ii].34. [500.]*
— Supplement A. 1954. ff.10. [125.]*

CANADIAN theses. A list of theses accepted by
canadian universities. National library of Canada:
Ottawa.
  1952. pp.[iv].50.4. [1250.]
no more published.

RESEARCH on immigrant adjustment and ethnic
groups. A bibliography of unpublished theses
1920-1953. Canadian citizenship branch: Ottawa
1955. pp.[ii].ii.131. [650.]*

Cuba

ELENA LUISA VÉREZ DE PERAZA, Publicaciones de
las institutiones culturales cubanas. Biblioteca del
bibliotecario (no.29): Habana 1949. ff.viii.149.
[613.]
  100 copies reproduced from typewriting.
— — Segunda edición. 1954. ff.vii.247. [924.]

Academic Writings

Denmark

[SVEND DAHL], Danish theses for the doctorate and commemorative publications of the university of Copenhagen, 1836–1926. A bio-bibliography. Copenhagen &c. 1929. pp.xvi.395. [1250.]

[—] — Danish theses for the doctorate 1927–1958. A bibliography. Library research monographs (vol.6): 1962. pp.xv.249. [1389.]

Finland, see also *Sweden*

OTTO E[DUARD] A[UGUST] HJELT, Det finnska universitets disputatians- och program-litteratur unde åren 1828–1908. Helsingfors 1909. pp.vii.162. [1800.]

France

P[IERRE] SUË, Tables chronologique et alphabétiques des thèses in-8° soutenues à l'Ecole de médecine de Paris . . . depuis le 28 frimaire an VII jusques et compris le 6 floréal an XII. 1806. pp.vii.80. [406.]

BULLETIN bibliographique des sociétés savantes des départements, contenant l'indication de leurs travaux et celle des publications individuelles qui paraissent en province. 1re année [*sic*]. — 1er vo-

Writings*

lume. Institut des provinces de France: 1851–
1853. pp.350. [488.]
no more published.

[LOUIS] ATH[ÉNAÏS] MOURIER, Notice sur le
doctorat ès lettres, suivie du catalogue des thèses
latines et françaises admises par les facultés des
lettres depuis 1810. 1852. pp.66. [300.]
—— Quatrième édition. Par A. Mourier et
F[élix] Deltour. 1880 [1881]. pp.[iii].xii.442.
[2000.]
——— [supplements]. Catalogue et analyse
des thèses françaises et latines [1890–1891 —
1901–1902: latines et françaises] admises par les
facultés des lettres.
    1880–1881. pp.x.36. [23.]
    1881–1882. pp.iii–viii.32. [13.]
    1882–1883. pp.vi.26. [19.]
    1883–1884. pp.[iv].39. [19.]
    1884–1885. pp.[iv].32. [16.]
    1885–1886. pp.[iv].42. [17.]
    1886–1887. pp.[iv].56. [21.]
    1887–1888. pp.[iv].40. [21.]
    1888–1889. Par F. Deltour et S[iméon] Ber-
      nage. pp.[iv].36. [18.]
    1889–1890. Par F. Deltour. pp.[iv].32. [17.]
    1890–1891. pp.[iv].48. [26.]

1891–1892. pp.[iv].56. [26.]
1892–1893. pp.[iv].56. [24.]
1893–1894. pp.48. [24.]
1894–1895. pp.64. [22.]
1895–1896. pp.64. [29.]
1896–1897. pp.52. [23.]
1897–1898. pp.84. [30.]
[*continued as:*]
Recueil Mourier-Deltour. Catalogue [&c.].
1898–1899. pp.80. [24.]
1899–1900. pp.68. [18.]
1900–1901. pp.124. [27.]
1901–1902. pp.92. [29.]
no more published.

[LOUIS] ATH[ÉNAÏS] MOURIER, Notice sur le doctorat ès sciences, suivie du catalogue des thèses admises par les facultés des sciences depuis 1810. 1856. pp.79. [300.]

[COUNT] A[DOLPHE CHARLES THÉODORE] DE FONTAINE DE RESBECQ, Notice sur le doctorat en droit, avec . . . une analyse chronologique des lois, statuts, décrets . . . relatifs à cet enseignement, de 1791 à 1857, suivie . . . du catalogue raisonné des thèses soutenues de 1851 à 1857. 1857. pp.[iii]. lxiii.199. [500.]

[LOUIS EUGÈNE F[ERDINAND] POUY, Iconographie

Academic Writings

des thèses. Notice sur les thèses dites historiées soutenues ou gravées, notamment par des Picards. Amiens 1869. pp.44. [30.]

CATALOGUE des thèses et écrits académiques. Ministère de l'instruction publique [l'éducation nationale].

    i. 1884–1889.[1885–]1892.pp.[iii].275.[4500.]

    ii. 1889–1894. [1890–]1894. pp.[iii].301. [5000.]

    corrections by G. Zedler appear in the Central-blatt für bibliothekswesen *(Leipzig 1894), xi. 516–519.*

    iii. 1894–1899. [1895–]1899. pp.[iii].coll.932. [8500.]

    iv. 1899–1904. [1900–]1904. pp.[iii].coll.1122. [10,000.]

    v. 1904–1909. [1905–]1910. pp.[iii].coll.1014. [9000.]

    vi. 1909–1913. [1910–1915]. pp.[iii].coll.972. [9000.]

    vii. 1914–1918. 1919. pp.[iii].coll.410. [4000.]

    viii. 1919–1923.1925.pp.[iii].coll.882.pp.883–973. [10,000.]

fasc.

    xli. 1924. 1927. coll.184. [2000.]

    xlii. 1925. 1928. coll.192. [2100.]

xliii. 1926. 1929. coll.200. [2200.]
xliv. 1927. 1930. coll.190. [2100.]
xlv. 1928. 1932. coll.180. [2000.]
xlvi. 1929. 1933. coll.198. [2200.]
xlvii. 1930. 1933. pp.95. [2100.]
xlviii. 1931. 1934. pp.95. [2100.]
xlix. 1932. 1935. pp.109. [2400.]
l. 1933. 1936. pp.112. [2500.]
li. 1934. 1937. pp.120. [2600.]
lii. 1935. 1938. coll.241–502. [2500.]
liii. 1936. 1939. pp.[i].126. [2500.]
liv. 1937. 1940. pp.[i].128. [2500.]
lv. 1938. 1941. pp.[i].124. [2500.]
lvi. 1939. 1944. pp.[i].171. [3500.]
lvii. 1940. 1948. pp.173–266. [2000.]
lviii. 1941. 1949. pp.[i].267–346. [1800.]
lviii [*sic*, lix]. 1942. 1949. pp.[i].347–428.
   [1800.]
lx. 1943. 1950. pp.[i].429–518. [1800.]
lxi. 1944. 1950. pp.[i].91. [2000.]
lxii. 1945. 1950. pp.92–215. [2200.]
lxiii. 1946. 1951. pp.216–332. [2200.]
lxiv. 1947. 1951. pp.[i].333–454. [2500.]
lxv. 1948. 1952. pp.[i].455–589. [2800.]
lxvi. 1949. 1952. pp.[i].135. [2500.]
lxvii. 1950. 1952. pp.136–277. [3000.]
lxviii. 1951. 1953. pp.278–450. [4000.]

lxix. 1952. 1954. pp.[i].451–622. [3500.]
lxx. 1953. pp.[i].623–804. [3500.]
lxxi. 1954. pp.[i].192. [4000.]
lxxii. 1955. pp.[i].193–392. [4000.]
lxxiii. 1956. pp.[i].393–585. [3821.]
lxxiv. 1957. pp.586–810. [3959.]
lxxv. 1958. pp.[i].811–1044. [3994.]
[*continued as:*]

Catalogue des thèses de doctorat soutenues devant les universités françaises. Nouvelle série. Direction des bibliothèques de France.
1959. pp.[i].377. [4032.]
1960. pp.[i].376. [4147.]
1961. pp.

in progress; the issues for 1940 &c. were also issued as Bibliographie de la France: supplément D.

[A. GIRARDIN], Liste des thèses du doctorat ès lettres qui se trouvent à la Bibliothèque universitaire de Poitiers. 1888. pp.xi–xxi. [1000.]

ALBERT MAIRE, Catalogue des thèses de sciences soutenues en France de 1810 à 1890 inclusivement. Bibliographie des thèses (no.2): 1892. pp.xi.224. [1000.]
—— Revue décennale des thèses présentées à la Faculté des sciences de Paris en vue du grade de docteur ès sciences du 1er janvier 1891 au

31 décembre 1900, avec l'indication des périodiques contenant la plupart de ces mémoires. Par E[ugène Pierre] Estanave. Arcis-sur-Aube 1901. pp.115. [347.]

PAUL [MARIE JEAN] DORVEAUX, Catalogue des thèses de pharmacie soutenues en province . . . (1803–1894), suivi d'un appendice du "Catalogue des thèses . . . de Paris". 1894. pp.117. [800.]

CATALOGUE mensuel des thèses soutenues devant les universités françaises. Bibliothèque universitaire: Montpellier 1898 &c.

EUGÈNE [PIERRE] ESTANAVE, Nomenclature des mémoires de physique expérimentale et de physique mathématique présentés en France dans le courant du XIXe siècle devant les facultés des sciences en vue du doctorat. 1903. pp.20. [300.]

E[UGÈNE PIERRE] ESTANAVE, Nomenclature des thèses de sciences mathématiques soutenues en France dans le courant du XIXe siècle devant les facultés des sciences de Paris et des départements. 1903. pp.viii.44. [292.]

ALBERT MAIRE, Répertoire alphabétique des thèses de doctorat ès lettres des universités françaises, 1810–1900. 1903. pp.vi.227. [2182.]

V[ICTOR] LIEUTAUD, Une Pléiade nouvelle du

ciel bas-alpin. Digne [printed] [1908]. pp.12. [50.]
*a bibliography of doctoral theses by natives of the
Basses-Alpes.*

CATALOGUE des thèses de droit soutenues devant
les facultés de France. Université de Paris: Faculté
de droit: 1933 &c.

CHARLES THOMAS, Répertoire méthodique des
thèses françaises d'ophtalmologie soutenues de
1904 à 1937. Laboratoire des tubes Dulcis:
Montecarlo [1938]. pp.36. [1300.]

L[UCIEN] CAES and R[OGER] HENRION, Collectio
bibliographica operum ad ius romanum pertinentium. Series II. Theses. Vol.1. Theses Galliae.
Bruxelles 1950. pp.3–447. [6000.]

[ÉMILE POULAT], Thèses et mémoires présentés en
France de 1940 à 1954 et touchant à la sociologie
des religions. Centre national de la recherche scientifique: Archives de sociologie des religions: 1956.
pp.13. [180.]

[ÉMILE POULAT], Soixante-dix ans d'études asso-
ciationnistes. Les thèses universitaires françaises,
1885–1955. Archives internationales de sociologie
de la coopération (1957, no.1): Aubenas [printed]
1957. pp.176–204+183–216. [383.]

Academic Writings

Germany

[JOHANN MARTIN BURGMANN], Nova literaria, quæ disputationes aliasque commentatiunculas theologcais, juridicas, medicas et philosophicas in præcipuis Germaniæ academiis et gymnasiis novissime evulgatas, recensent. Lipsiæ 1727. pp.200. [500.]

almost wholly limited to the publications of the year 1726–1727.

[CONRAD KOCH, *called* WIMPINA], Scriptorum insignium, qvi in celeberrimis præsertim Lipsiensi, Wittenbergensi, Franfordiana ad Oderam academiis, a fundatione ipsarum, usque ad annum Christi 1515. floruerunt, ccnturia, ab avctore eivs temporis anonymo concinnata, nunc vero in lucem edita, à Joachimo Johanne Madero. Helmaestadi 1660. pp.[76]. [500.]

[—] — Ex mspto autographo . . . luci publicae tradita a J[ohann] Fr[iedrich] L[udwig] Theod[or] Merzdorf. Lipsiae 1839. pp.100. [500.]

CARL JOHANN FOGEL, Bibliotheca hamburgensis tripartita, nempe theologico-medico-philosophica, comprehendens disputationes, a viris, Hamburgi natis . . . habitas. Hamburgi 1732. pp.[ii].78. [1000.]

Academic Writings

JOHANNES VON GRUBER, Verzeichniss sämmtlicher abhandlungen in den auf preussischen gymnasien erschienenen programmen von 1825–1837. Berlin 1840. pp.vi[*sic*, iv].36. [1250.]

JOSEPH GUTENÄCKER, Verzeichniss aller programme und gelegenheitsschriften, welche an den k. b. studien-anstalten vom schuljahre 1823/24 bis zum schlusse des schuljahres 1841/42 erschienen sind. Würzburg 1843. pp.iv.56. [481.]

— — 1823/24–1859/60. Bamberg 1862. pp.viii. 165. [1500.]

[F. WINIEWSKI], Systematisches verzeichniss der in den programmen der preussischen gymnasien und progymnasien welche in den jahren 1825–1841 erschienen sind, enthaltenen abhandlungen, reden und gedichte. Münster 1844. pp.xvi.102. [2000.]

— — Systematisch geordnetes verzeichnis der abhandlungen, reden und gedichte, die in den an den preussischen gymnasien 1842–1850 erschienenen programmen enthalten sind; von Gustav Hahn. Salzwedel 1854. pp.[ii].iv.50. [1250.]

— — — 1851–1860. Salzwedel 1864. pp.viii. 62. [1250.]

Academic Writings

PH. A. F. WALTHER, Systematisches repertorium über die schriften sämmtlicher historischen gesellschaften Deutschlands. Darmstadt 1845. pp.xxx.649. [7000.]

PROGRAMMENREVUE oder schul-archiv. . . . Herausgegeben von A. R. Albani.

    i. 1843. 1846. pp.xxvi.360.[x].72. [250.]

    ii (no.1). 1844–1846. 1847. pp.xii.52. [25.]
no more published.

VERZEICHNIS der programme und gelegenheitsschriften welche an den bayer. lyceen, gymnasien und latein-schulen sowie an anderen mittelschulen . . . erschienen sind. Bamberg.

    [i]. 1823–1860. Von Joseph Gutenäcker. [1860.]

    ii. 1860–1873. Von J[ohann] G[eorg] Zeiss.

    iii. 1873–1884.

    iv. 1884–1889. Von E[mil] Renn.

    v. 1889–1895.

    vi. 1895–1902.

S. CALVARY & CO., Die schul-programme und dissertationen . . . nebst einem verzeichniss der im Jahre 1863 erschienenen programme und dissertationen. Berlin 1864. pp.28. [967.]

—— Verzeichniss der im jahre 1864 erschie-

nenen universitäts- und schul-schriften. 1865.
pp.[iv].31. [1191.]

— — — 1865. 1867. pp.viii.42. [1251.]
limited to german and austrian publications.

FRANZ HÜBL, Systematisch-geordnetes verzeichniss derjenigen abhandlungen, reden, gedichte u. d. g., welche in den mittelschulpro-
grammen Oesterreich-Ungarns seit d. j. 1850 bis
1869 und in jenen von Preussen seit 1852 und
von Baiern seit 1863 bis 1868 enthalten sind.
Czernowitz 1869. pp.240. [5000.]

HERMANN VARNHAGEN, Systematisches verzeichniss der auf die neueren sprachen, hauptsächlich
die französische und englische, sowie die sprach-
wissenschaft überhaupt bezüglichen programm-
abhandlungen, dissertationen und habilitationsschriften. Leipzig 1877. pp.[iii]. iv.xix.100. [1750.]
also issued as a supplement to Bernhardt Schmitz,
Encyclopädie des philologischen studiums der
neueren sprachen, *Greifswald &c. 1859–1877.*

— — Zweite . . . auflage. Besorgt von Johannes
Martin. 1893. pp.xvi.296. [4000.]

RUDOLF KLUSSMANN, Systematisches verzeichnis
der abhandlungen welche in den schulschriften
sämtlicher an dem programmaustausche teilneh-

menden lehranstalten erschienen sind. Leipzig. 1876–1885. 1889. pp.viii.316. [5000.]

> *authors' names are given with initials only and some of these are amplified by E[rnst Carl Ferdinand] Roth in the* Centralblatt für bibliothekswesen *(1892), ix. 376–378, 430, 524–525, (1893), x. 364–365, 502–503.*

1886–1890. 1893. pp.vii.285. [4000.]

1891–1895. 1899. pp.vii.342. [4500.]

1896–1900. 1903. pp.viii.348. [4500.]

1901–1910. 1916. pp.x.584. [7500.]

no more published.

JAHRES-VERZEICHNISS der an den deutschen universitäten [vols. xxix–xxxix: und technicshen hochschulen: xl–li: und hochschulen] erschienenen schriften. Berlin.

> i. 1885–1886. pp.[iv].238. [1750.]
>
> ii. 1886–1887. pp.[ii].268]. [2000.]
>
> iii. 1887–1888. pp.[iv].301. [2250.]
>
> iv. 1888–1889. pp.[iii].310. [2250.]
>
> v. 1889–1890. pp.[iii].321. [2500.]
>
> —Sach-register zu i.–v. 1891. pp.96.
>
> vi. 1890–1891. pp.[v].355. [2750.]
>
> vii. 1891–1892. pp.[iii].317. [2500.]
>
> viii. 1892–1893. pp.[iii].315. [2750.]
>
> ix. 1893–1894. pp.[iii].304. [2500.]

x. 1894–1895. pp.[iii].310. [2500.]

xi. 1895–1896. pp.[iii].344. [2750.]

xii. 1896–1897. pp.[iii].361. [3000.]

xiii. 1897–1898. pp.[v].321. [2750.]

xiv. 1898–1899. pp.[iii].327. [2750.]

xv. 1899–1900. pp.[iii].312. [2500.]

xvi. 1900–1901. pp.[iii].372. [3000.]

xvii. 1901–1902. pp.[iii].434. [3750.]

xviii. 1902–1903. pp.[iii].479. [4000.]

xix. 1903–1904. [By Adalbert Hortzschan-
sky]. pp.[iii].496. [4000.]

xx. 1904–1905. pp.[iv].668. [3500.]

xxi. 1905–1906. pp.[iv].673. [3500].

xxii. 1906–1907. [By — Kopp.] pp.[iv].728.
[3500.]

xxiii. 1907–1908. pp.[v].759. [3750.]

xxiv. 1908–1909. [By — Jahr.] pp.[v].826.
[4000.]

xxv. 1909–1910. pp.[v].878. [4500.]

xxvi. 1910–1911. pp.[v].919. [4500.]

xxvii. 1911–1912. pp.[v].955. [4750.]

xxviii. 1912. pp.[v].478. [2250.]

xxix. 1913. pp.[v].990. [5000.]

xxx. 1914. pp.[v].994. [5000.]

xxxi. 1915. pp.[v].522. [2500.]

xxxii. 1916. pp.[v].446. [2250.]

xxxiii. 1917. pp.[v].401. [2000.]

xxxiv. 1918. pp.[v].366. [1750.]

xxxv. 1919. pp.[v].548. [2750.]

xxxvi. 1920. pp.[v].852. [4000.]

xxxvii. 1921. pp.[v].1589. [7500.]

xxxviii. 1922. pp.[v].1175. [11,000.]

xxxix. 1923. pp.[v].1291. [11,500.]

xl. 1924. pp.[v].1200. [10,000.]

xli. 1925. pp.[v].1185. [9250.]

xlii. 1926. pp.[v].1023. [8000.]

xliii. 1927. pp.[v].867. [6500.]

xliv. 1928. pp.[iv].977. [7250.]

xlv. 1929. pp.[iv].868. [6750.]

xlvi. 1930. pp.[iv].974. [7500.]

xlvii. 1931. pp.[vi].982. [9000.]

xlviii. 1932. pp.[iii].xi.945. [8750.]

xlix. 1933. pp.xi.955. [7750.]

l. 1934. pp.xi.1036. [8500.]

li. 1935. pp.[v].1125. [9250.]

[*continued as:*]

Jahresverzeichnis der deutschen Hochschulschriften. Bearbeitet von der Deutschen bücherei.

lii. 1936. pp.[v].892. [10,022.]

liii. 1937. [By Hans Praesent]. pp.[v].870.
[9951.]

liv. 1938. pp.[v].838. [9397.]

lv. 1939. pp.[v].836. [9212.]

lvi. 1940. pp.xii.680. [7110.]

lvii. 1941. pp.xii.568. [5991.]
lviii–lx. 1942–1944.
lxi–lxiv. 1945–1948. pp.viii.1092. [12,950.]
lxv. 1949. pp.viii.652. [7348.]
lxvi. 1950. pp.viii.725. [7732.]
lxvii. 1951. pp.viii.928. [9276.]
lxviii. 1952. pp.viii.1006. [9028.]
lxix. 1953. pp.viii.1038. [9135.]
lxx. 1954. pp.viii.1067. [8931.]
lxxi. 1955. pp.viii.1024. [8804.]
lxxii. 1956. pp.viii.1096.41. [8417.]
lxxiii. 1957. pp.viii.45.1128. [8716.]
lxxiv. 1958. pp.viii.57.950. [7924.]
lxxv. 1959. pp.51.722. [8028.]

lxxvi. 1960. pp.viii.69.1065. [8577.]
in progress.

RICHARD [CORNELIUS WILHELM] KUKULA, All-
gemeiner deutscher hochschulen-almanach. Wien
1888. pp.vi.1000. [35,000.]
— — [another edition]. Bibliographisches jahrbuch der deutschen hochschulen. Innsbruck 1892.
pp.iv.1071. [40,000.]
— — — 1. Ergänzungsheft. 1893. pp.[iii].295.
[8000.]

JAHRES-VERZEICHNISS der an den deutschen

schulanstalten erschienenen abhandlungen. Berlin.

    i. 1889. pp.[v].48. [477.]
    ii. 1890. pp.[iii].82. [640.]
    iii. 1891. pp.[iii].89. [672.]
    iv. 1892. pp.[iii].68. [591.]
    v. 1893. pp.[iii].80. [713.]
    vi. 1894. pp.[iii].73. [648.]
    vii. 1895. pp.[iii].74. [646.]
    viii. 1896. pp.[iii].77. [670.]
    ix. 1897. pp.[iii].80. [683.]
    x. 1898. pp.[v].73. [652.]
    xi. 1899. pp.[iii].71. [619.]
    xii. 1900. pp.[iii].73. [629.]
    xiii. 1901. pp.[iii].73. [641.]
    xiv. 1902. pp.[iii].72. [589.]
    xv. 1903. pp.[iii].66. [538.]
    xvi. 1904. pp.[iii].52. [435.]
    xvii. 1905. pp.[iii].51. [434.]
    xviii. 1906. pp.[iii].49. [431.]
    xix. 1907. pp.[iii].60. [474.]
    xx. 1908. pp.[iv].66. [553.]
    xxi. 1909. pp.[iii].70. [523.]
    xxii. 1910. pp.[iii].63. [491.]
    xxiii. 1911. pp.[iii].72. [547.]
    xxiv. 1912. pp.[iii].66. [496.]
    xxv. 1913. pp.[iii].74. [571.]
    xxvi. 1914. pp.[iii].68. [489.]

xxvii. 1915. pp.[iii].31. [212.]

xxviii. 1916–1930. Staatsbibliothek: 1931.
pp.[v].242. [2174.]

*no more published; authors' names are given with
initials only and some of these are amplified by E[rnst
Carl Ferdinand] Roth in the* Centralblatt für biblio-
thekswesen *(1892), ix. 288–289, and by R[udolf]
Klussmann, ibid. (1897), xiv. 137–139; (1898), xv.
431–433.*

VERZEICHNISS der seit 1850 an den deutschen
universitäten erschienenen doctor-dissertationen
und habilitationsschriften aus der reinen und
angewandten mathematik. Deutsche mathematikvereinigung: München 1893. pp.[iii].35.
[1500.]

WILHELM ERMAN and EWALD HORN, Bibliographie der deutschen universitäten. Systematisch
geordnetes verzeichnis der bis ende 1899 gedruck-
ten bücher und aufsätze über das deutsche univer-
sitätswesen. Leipzig &c. 1904–1905. pp.xx.836+
xx.1236+v.313. [40,000.]

G. ZIELER and TH. SCHEFFER, Das akademische
Deutschland. Biographisch-bibliographisches
handbuch für die universitäten des Deutschen
reiches, als ergänzung zum Deutschen universitäts-

kalender. Leipzig 1905–1906. pp.viii.83+[ii].iv.86
+317. [7500.]
incomplete; no more published.

RICHARD ULLRICH, Programmwesen und pro-
grammbibliothek der höheren schulen in Deutschland, Österreich und der Schweiz. . . . Mit pro-
grammbibliographie und einem verzeichnis aus-
gewählter programme von 1824–1906 (1907).
Berlin 1908. pp.xxiv.81–767. [4000.]

HANS LEY, Verzeichnis sämtlicher programme,
welche an den Kgl. bayer. real- und oberreal-
schulen (ehemaligen landwirtschafts- und ge-
werbeschulen) vom jahre 1833 bis 1912 inkl.
erschienen sind. Nürnberg 1913. pp.62. [1150.]
also issued as a supplement to the Jahresbericht *for
1912–1913 of the Kreisrealschule of Nürnberg.*

PAUL TROMMSDORFF, Verzeichnis der bis ende
1912 an den technischen hochschulen des Deutschen reiches erschienenen schriften. Berlin 1914.
pp.x.184. [2972.]

WALTER CARTELLIERI, Verzeichnis der Saar-
dissertationen. Berlin 1933. pp.24.

ELISBATH BOEDEKER, 25 Jahre frauenstudium in
Deutschland. Verzeichnis der doktorarbeiten von

frauen, 1908–1933. Hannover 1935–1939.
details of this work are set out under Women, below.

DIE WIRTSCHAFTSWISSENSCHAFTLICHEN hochschularbeiten. Institut für angewandte wirtschafts-
wissenschaft: Berlin [1936]. pp.vii.310. [2500.]

FR[ITZ] FRANZMEYER, Presse-dissertationen an
deutschen hochschulen, 1885–1938. . . . Herausgegeben von Walter Heide. Leipzig 1940. pp.167.
[1353.]

LUTZ RÖHRICH, Bibliographie volkskundlicher
dissertationen an deutschen universitäten, 1945–
1950. Stuttgart 1951. pp.18. [214.]*

BIBLIOGRAPHIE der landwirtschaftlichen hochschulschriften . . . in deutscher sprache . . . auf dem
gebiet der land- und forstwirtschaftswissenschaften. Deutsche bücherei: Sonderbibliographien
(no.1 &c.]: Leipzig.
    1945–1952. [Edited by] Werner Dux, Curt
        Fleischhack. . . . (no.1). pp.xii.172. [1992.]
    1953–1956. . . . (no.14). pp.xii.339. [3452.]
in progress.

RICHARD MUMMENDEY, Die sprache und literatur
der Angelsachsen im spiegel der deutschen universitätsschriften, 1885–1950. Eine bibliographie.

[Bonner beiträge zur bibliotheks- und bücherkunde (vol.1)]: Bonn 1954. pp.xvi.200. [2989.]

HOCHSCHULSCHRIFTEN zur neueren deutschen
geschichte. Eine bibliographie. Kommission für
geschichte des parlamentarismus und der politischen parteien: Bonn.

 i. 1945–1955. Von Alfred Milatz und Thilo
  Vogelsang. pp.3–142. [2325.]

BIBLIOGRAPHIE des handwerks. Verzeichnis der
dissertationen. Universität Göttingen: Seminar
für handwerkswesen: Göttingen.*

 1943–1944. Bearbeitet von Marianne Kidery.
  1956. ff.147. [953.]
 1945–1952. Bearbeitet von Gerhard Kämpf.
  1955. ff.[48]. [300.]

GISELA SCHWANBECK, Bibliographie der deutsch-
sprachigen hochschulschriften zur theaterwissenschaft von 1885 bis 1952. Gesellschaft für theatergeschichte: Schriften (vol.58): Berlin 1956. pp.
xiv.566. [3309.]*

HOCHSCHULARBEITEN aus agrarökonomik und
agrarsoziologie. Bibliographie abgeschlossener
und laufender dissertationen. Forschungsgesellschaft für agrarpolitik und agrarsoziologie (no.
63 &c.): Bonn 1957 &c.*

in progress; details of this work are entered under Agriculture, below.

[HANS FLASCHE], Die sprachen und literaturen der Romanen im spiegel der deutschen universitätsschriften, 1885–1950. Bonner beiträge zur bibliotheks- und bücherkunde (vol.iii): Bonn 1958. pp.xxii.299. [4688.]
also issued by the Bibliographical society of the university of Virginia under the title of Romance languages and literatures *(Charlottesville).*

FRITZ MEYEN, Die nordeuropäischen länder im spiegel der deutschen universitätsschriften, 1885–1957. Bonner beiträge zur bibliotheks- und bücherkunde (vol.iv): Bonn 1958. pp.xxii.126. [1099.]
also issued under the title of The north european nations.

DIE VÖLKERRECHTLICHEN dissertationen an den westdeutschen universitäten 1945–1957. Deutsche gesellschaft für völkerrecht: Karlsruhe 1958. pp.52. [500.]

HANS FLASCHE and UTTA WAWRZINEK, Materialien zur begriffsgeschichte. Eine bibliographie deutscher hochschulschriften von 1900–1955. Ar-

chiv für begriffsgeschichte (vol.5): Bonn 1960.
pp.xix.718. [9491.]

URSULA WEIDIG, Bibliographie der dissertationen aus körperkultur, körpererziehung, sport und
verwandten gebieten. In- und ausländische dissertationen in deutscher sprache sowie an deutschen
universitäten verteidigte fremdsprachige dissertationen von 1648 bis 1959. Mit einem anhang:
habilitationsschriften. Deutsche hochschule für
körperkultur: Bibliothek: Sportbibliographien
(no.6): Leipzig 1960. pp.128.

HANS BERNDT and SIEGFRIED GÜNTHER, Bibliographie der deutschen hochschulschriften zur
chemie. Ein systematisches verzeichnis der in den
jahren 1957–1958 an deutschen universitäten und
hochschulen eingereichten dissertationen und
habilitationsschriften. Deutsche bücherei: Sonderbibliographien (no.23): Leipzig 1960. pp.viii.264.
[2631.]

KLAUS LUDWIG JANERT, Verzeichnis indienkundlicher hochschulschriften: Deutschland, Österreich, Schweiz. Wiesbaden 1961. pp.ix.80. [931.]

JOCHEN KÖHLER, Deutsche dissertationen über
Afrika. Ein verzeichnis für die jahre 1918–1959.

Deutsche Afrika-gesellschaft: Bonn 1962. pp. [249]. [795.]*

HANS JÜRGEN ROJEK, Bibliographie der deutsch-sprachigen hochschulschriften zur theaterwissenschaft von 1953 bis 1960. Gesellschaft für theatergeschichte: Schriften (vol.61): Berlin 1962. pp. xvi.170. [558.]*

RICHARD SCHAAL, Verzeichnis deutschsprachiger musikwissenschaftlicher dissertationen, 1861–1960. Gesellschaft für musikforschung: Musikwissenschaftliche arbeiten (no.19): Kassel 1963. pp.167. [2819.]

Great Britain

A[BRAHAM] HUME, The learned societies and printing clubs of the United Kingdom ... with ... their published works and transactions. 1847. pp.xxxii.308. [750.]

—— With a supplement containing all the recently-established societies and clubs . . . by A. I. Evans. 1853. pp.xxxii.308.72. [750.]

BULLETIN of the Institute of historical research. Theses supplement. 1933 &c.

in progress; details of this work are entered under History, below.

A[NNIE] M[ARGARET] BLACKWELL, A list of

researches in education and educational psychology presented for higher degrees in the universities of the United Kingdom, northern Ireland, and the Irish Republic from 1918 to 1948. National foundation for educational research in England and Wales: [1950]. pp.173. [2250.]

— — A second list . . . 1949, 1950, and 1951. 1952. pp.127. [1000.]

— — Supplement for . . . 1952 and 1953. [1954]. pp.62. [600.]

INDEX to theses accepted for higher degrees in the universities of Great Britain and Ireland. Aslib [Association of special libraries and information bureaux].

> i. 1950–1951. Edited by P[eter] D[ouglas] Record. pp.xii.157. [2182.]
> ii. 1951–1952. Edited by P. D. Record and Magda Whitrow. pp.xii.175. [3040.]
> iii. 1952–1953. Edited by M. Whitrow. pp.xi.159. [2686.]
> iv. 1953–1954. pp.xii.158. [2565.]
> v. 1954–1955. pp.xii.170. [2754.]
> vi. 1955–1956. pp.xii.165. [2713.]
> vii. 1956–1957. pp.xii.177. [2850.]
> viii. 1957–1958. pp.xii.173. [2918.]
> ix. 1958–1959. pp.xii.172. [3129.]

x.1959–1960. pp.xii.188. [3189.]
xi. 1960–1961. pp.xii.183. [3206.]
in progress.

F. NORMAN, *ed.* Theses in germanic studies . . .
(excluding english), approved for higher degrees
in the university of Great Britain and Ireland between 1903 and 1961. University of London:
Institute of germanic languages and literatures:
1962. pp.viii.46. [455.]

India

BIBLIOGRAPHY of doctorate theses in science and
arts accepted by indian universities. Inter-uni-
versity board of India: Mitijhil [&c.] 1930–1934.

G[IRIRAJ] P[RASAD] GUPTA, Economic investigations in India. (A bibliography of researches in
commerce and economics approved by indian
universities). Agra [1961]. pp.[iii].v.81. [750.]

Italy

G. B. CAO-MASTIO, Indice dei discorsi inaugurali
letti nelle R. università del regno dal 1876–77 al
1888–89. Roma 1890. pp.50. [218.]

[GIULIO PROVENZAL], Profusioni di argomento
scientifico lette nelle università e negli istituti
superiori d'Italia per la inaugurazione dell'anno

scolastico dal 1860 al 1930. Consiglio nazionale delle ricerche: Roma 1932. pp.viii.150.

Netherlands

J[ENS] J[ENSEN] DODT, Repertorium dissertationum belgicarum, sive index ... omnium dissertationum inauguralium, quae ab anno MDCCCXV. usque ad annum MDCCCXXX. auspiciis academiarum belgicarum sunt impressae. Trajecti ad Rhenum [1835]. pp.[iv].19.17.23.16.30.17.26. [2750.]

a supplement by Jean Pie Namur appears in the Bibliophile belge *(1848), v. 113–118.*

[WILLEM NIKOLAAS DU RIEU], Register van academische dissertatien en oratien betreffende de geschiedenis des vaderlands. Maatschappij der nederlandsche letterkunde: Commissie voor geschied- en outheidkunde: Leiden 1886. pp.[iii]. iv.104. [1601.]

—— Supplement. 1882. pp.[viii].47. [800.]

CATALOGUE d'une collection de thèses publiées dans les Pays-Bas donnée à la Bibliothèque nationale par le Service des échanges internationaux. 1884–1885. pp.69+49. [3000.]

THÈSES de droit soutenues aux universités des Pays-Bas 1700–1898 [*on cover:* Catalogus disser-

tationum iuridicarum defensarum in academiis
Neerlandiae]. Leyde 1898. pp.[iv].151.

M. A. DÉE, Academische proefschriften verdedigd te Leiden, Utrecht, Groningen en Amsterdam in der jaren 1877–1899. Leiden 1900.
pp.[vii].167. [2866.]

J. W. WIJNDELTS, Catalogus van academische
proefschriften, verdedigd van de nederlandsche
universiteiten gedurende de jaren 1815–1900.
Groningen 1901-1903. pp.[iii].52+[iii].70.[1076.]
parts i and v only; no more published.

CATALOGUS van academische geschriften in
Nederland en nederlandsch Indië verschenen.
Nederlandsche vereeniging van bibliothecarissen
en bibliotheekambtenaren [iv &c.: van bibliothe-
carissen]: Utrecht [iv &c.: 's-Gravenhage].

   i. 1924. pp.[ii].23. [200.]
   ii. 1925. pp.[iii].21–46.[iv]. [200.]
   iii. 1926. pp.[ii].47–71.[iii]. [200.]
   iv. 1927. pp.[ii].73–102.[iv]. [250.]
   v. 1928. pp.[ii].103-133.[iv]. [250.]
   — 1924–1928. Naam- en zaakregister. 1930.
      pp.[ii].135–186.
   vi. 1929. pp.[ii].137–169.[iv]. [300.]
   vii. 1930. pp.[ii].171–203.[iv.] [300.]

viii. 1931. pp.[ii].205–238.[iv]. [300.]
ix. 1932. pp.[ii].239–275.[iv]. [350.]
x. 1933. pp.[ii].277–314.[v]. [400.]
— 1924–1933. Naam- en zachregister. 1934.
xi. 1934. pp.39.[iv]. [372.]
xii. 1935. pp.[ii].41–76.[iv]. [377.]
xiii. 1936. pp.[ii].77–112.[iv]. [382.]
xiv. 1937. pp.[ii].113–148.[iv]. [360.]
xv. 1938. pp.[ii].149–190.[v]. [452.]
xvi. 1939. pp.[ii].191–222.[iv]. [355.]
xvii. 1940. pp.[i].223–250.[iii]. [291.]
xviii–xxii. 1941–1945. pp.103. [941.]
[*continued as:*]

Catalogus van academische geschriften in Nederland verschenen.
xxiii–xxvi. 1946–1949. 1952. pp.166. [1561].
xxvii–xxviii. 1950–1951. 1954. pp.89. [750.]
xxix–xxx. 1952–1953. 1958. pp.84. [640.]
in progress.

CATALOGUS van proefschriften vervaardigd ter verkrijging van de graad van doctor in één der natuurwetenschappen in de jaren 1900–1930. [*s.l.*] 1931. pp.206.

Poland

KATALOG rozpraw doktorskich i habilitacynych.

Academic Writings

Ministerstwo szkolnictwa wýrszego: Warszawa.
1959–1961. pp.639. [3307.]
in progress.

Russia

N[IKOLAI P[ETROVICH] PETROV, Библіографическій указатель русскихъ диссертацій по медицинѣ и ветеринаріи... съ 1860 по 1-е іюня 1892 г. включительно. 2... изд. С.-Петербург 1892. pp.[ii].101. [2287.]

— — Дополненіе. 1896. pp.[ii].42. [1025.]

— — Второе дополненіе. 1898. pp.32. [617.]

ЕЖЕГОДНИК диссертаций. Всесоюзная книжная палата: Москва.
i. 1936. 1938. pp.180. [1321.]

БИБЛИОГРАФИЯ диссертации. Государственная... библиотека СССР им. В. И. Ленина: Москва.
1941–1944. 1946. pp.183. [559.]
1945. 1947. pp.103. [241.]

КАТАЛОГ кандидатских и докторских диссертаций, поступивших в Библиотеку имени В. И. Ленина и Государственную центральную научную медицинскую библиотеку. Москва.

i. 1956. Составитель А. А. Кондратьев. pp.198. [1505.]

ii. 1957. pp.224. [1598.]

КАТАЛОГ ДОКТОРСКИХ ДИССЕРТАЦИЙ, поступивших в библиотеку. Государственная . . . публичная библиотека СССР им. В. И. Ленина. Москва.

1956. Составитель Кондратьев А. А. pp.47. [304.]

[*continued as:*]

Каталог кандидатских диссертаций, поступивших в библиотеку . . . и Государственную центральную научную медицинскую библиотеку.

1957. pp.172+188. [3060.]

1958. pp.212+291. [3217.]

1959. pp.296+

1960. pp.196+188+243+263. [7360.]

1961. pp.   +   +267+   . [.]

[L. A. OSIPCNIK], Библиография диссертаций защищенных в Белорусской ССР за 1945–1955 годы. Академия наук БССР: Финдаментальная библиотека. Минск 1958. pp.88. [704.]

— дополнение [1958]. pp.7 [35.]

ПЕРЕЧЕНЬ важнейших научно-исследова-

тельских работ, выполняемых высшими
учебными заведениями в 1958 году. Общественные науки. Министерство высшего обра-
зования СССР: Научно-технический совет:
Москва 1958, pp.146. [1300.]

VLADISLAV ADOLFOVICH RAKHLEVSKY and
GEORGY IVANOVICH USHAKOV, Диссертации по
финансам, денежному обращению, кредиту,
бухгалтерскому учету и анализу хозяй-
ственной деятельности, защищенные на уче-
ную степень доктора и кандидата экономи-
ческих наук с 1939 по 1961 г. Библиографический указатель. Москва 1962. pp.112.
[1500.]

Scotland

P[ETER] J[OHN] ANDERSON, Notes on academic
theses. Aberdeen university: Studies (no.58):
Aberdeen 1912. pp.[iii].52. [75.]

Spain

JOSEF DE REZABAL Y UGARTE, Biblioteca de los
escritores que han sido individuos de los seis
colegios mayores: de San Ildefonso de la Universidad de Alcalá, de Santa Cruz de la de Valladolid,
de San Bartolomé, de Cuenca, San Salvador de

Academic Writings

Oviedo, y el del Arzobispo de la de Salamanca.
Madrid 1805. pp.xvi.473.54. [1500.]

CATÁLOGO de las publicaciones y tesis doctorales destinadas al cambio internacional de libros.
Universidad de Madrid: Biblioteca: Madrid 1934.
pp.65.

Sweden and Finland

JOH[AN] HENR[IK] LIDÉN, Catalogus disputationum, in academiis et gymnasiis Sveciæ, atque
etiam, a Svecis, extra patriam habitarum. Upsaliæ
1778–1780. pp.606+221+225+54+63. [15,000.]
— — Supplementa addidit Gabr[iel] Marklin.
1820. pp.[ii].117. [1000.]
— — Catalogus disputationum in academiis
Scandinaviae et Finlandiae Lidenianus continuatus a Gabr. Marklin. 1820. pp.[ii].iv.262+179+
102. [6000.]
— — Continuatus a Gabr. Marklin. 1856.
pp.[iv].207+[ii].120+[ii].88. [6000.]
the last supplements were reissued, Stockholm 1874.
— — Avandlingar ock program utgivna vid
svenska ock finska akademier ock skolor under
åren 1855–1890. Bibliografi af Askel G[ustav]
S[alomon] Josephson. Uppsala [1891–1897].
pp.viii.264+267–344. [3500.]
— — Akademiska afhandlingar vid Sveriges

universitet och högskolor läsåren 1890/91–
1909/10, jämte förteckning öfver svenskars akademiska afhandlingarvid utländska universitet under
samma tid. Bibliografi af Axel [Herman] Nelson.
Uppsala 1911[-1912]. pp.viii.150. [1000.]

CHRISTIAN HAMMER, Katalog öfver disputationes
... programmata ... indices prælectionum ...
oratione, etc. Stockholm 1895. pp.[iv].67. [24,137.]

S[AMUEL] E[RIK] MELANDER, Förteckning öfver
afhandlingar och uppsatser som ingå i eller med-
följa årsredogörelserna för rikets allmäna läroverk.
Lund.

    1858–1882. 1912. pp.v.78. [400.]
    1883–1909. 1909. pp.viii.95. [500.]

[AKSEL ANDERSSON], Catalogue de l'Exposition
suédoise de l'enseignement supérieur. Établisse-
ments d'enseignement supérieur et savants. Publications savantes. Exposition universelle de Paris:
Upsal 1900. pp.vii.103. [750.]

OTTO E[DVARD] A[UGUST] HJELT, Sveriges biologiska disputations-och program-literatur, 1700–
vårterminen 1910. Bidrag till kännedom af Finlands natur och folk (vol.lxx, no.1): Helsingfors
1911. pp.viii.210. [2250.]

JOHN [OTTO] TUNELD, Akademiska avhandlin-

gar vid sveriges universitet och högskolor, läsåren
1910/11–1939/40. Bibliografi. Lund 1945. pp.336.
[2000.]

Switzerland, see also *Germany*

VERZEICHNISS der programme. [*s.l.* 1881]. pp.21.

JAHRESVERZEICHNIS der schweizerischen universitätsschriften. Basel.

    [i]. 1897–1898. [By C. Chr. Bernoulli]. pp.iv.
      63. [400.]

    [ii]. 1898–1899. pp.59. [400.]

    [iii]. 1899–1900. pp.66. [400.]

    [iv]. 1900–1901. pp.80. [500.]

    [v]. 1901–1902. pp.86. [500.]

    [vi]. 1902–1903. pp.88. [500.]

    [vii]. 1903–1904. pp.104. [600.]

    [viii]. 1904–1905. pp.111. [600.]

    [ix]. 1905–1906. pp.110. [600.]

    [x]. 1906–1907. pp.113. [600.]

    [xi]. 1907–1908. pp.118. [600.]

    [xii]. 1908–1909. pp.142. [750.]

        [*continued as:*]

Jahresverzeichnis der schweizerischen hochschulschriften.

    [xiii]. 1909–1910. pp.[iv].147. [800.]

    [xiv]. 1910–1911. pp.[iii].144. [800.]

    [xv]. 1911–1912. Redaktion: Oeffentliche

bibliothek der universität Basel. pp.[iii].
134. [750.]

[xvi]. 1912–1913. pp.[iii].119. [600.]

[xvii]. 1913–1914. pp.[iii].126. [600.]

[xviii]. 1914–1915. pp.[iii].98. [500.]

[xix]. 1915–1916. pp.[iii].101. [500.]

[xx]. 1916–1917. pp.[iii].85. [516.]

[xxi]. 1917–1918. pp.[iii].84. [499.]

[xxii]. 1918–1919. pp.[iii].79. [500.]

[xxiii]. 1919–1920. pp. [iii].91. [549.]

[xxiv]. 1920–1921. pp.[iii].95. [582.]

[xxv]. 1921–1922. pp.[iii].110. [661.]

[xxvi]. 1922–1923. pp.[iii].130. [810.]

[xxvii]. 1923–1924. pp.[iv].92. [750.]

— Verfasser-register zu den jahrgängen
1897/98–1922/23. [By Martha Binz]. 1927.
pp.87.

[xxviii]. 1925. pp.[iv].99. [800.]

[xxix]. 1926. [Edited by Hans Lutz]. pp.[iv].
118. [1000.]

xxx. 1927. pp.[iv].103. [789.]

xxxi. 1928. pp.[iv].118. [894.]

xxxii. 1929. [Edited by Paul Scherrer and
Hans Zehntner.] pp.[iv].108. [813.]

xxxiii. 1930. [Edited by Hans Zehntner].
pp.[iv].119. [882.]

xxxiv. 1931. pp.[iv].104. [721.]

xxxv. 1932. pp.[iv].105. [728.]
xxxvi. 1933. pp.[iv].103. [728.]
xxxvii. 1934. pp.[iv].116. [853.]
xxxviii. 1935. pp.[iv].121. [867.]
xxxix. 1935–1936. pp.[iv].130. [960.]
xl. 1936–1937. pp.[iv].143. [1063.]
xli. 1937–1938. pp.[iv].132. [930.]
xlii. 1938–1939. pp.[iv].134. [933.]
xliii. 1939–1940. pp.[iv].112. [748.]
xliv. 1940–1941. pp. [iv].108. [731.]
xlv. 1941–1942. pp.[iv].117. [772.]
xlvi. 1942–1943. [Edited by Hilda Trog]. pp.[iv].128. [790.]
xlvii. 1943–1944. pp.[iv].124. [741.]
xlviii. 1944–1945. pp.[iv].137. [857.]
xlix. 1945–1946. pp.[iv].145. [882.]
l. 1946–1947. pp.[vi].134. [872.]
li. 1948. pp.[iv].160. [1008.]
lii. 1949. pp.[iii].170. [986.]
liii. 1950. pp.[iii].174. [1029.]
liv. 1951 pp.[iii].188. [1134.]
lv. 1952. pp.[iii].187. [1179.]
in progress.

United States

i. *Periodicals*

DIRECTORY of college media. New York [1957].

Academic Writings

pp.[iii].xxvii.177. [1750.]*

ii. *General*

THOMAS R[OSSMAN] PALFREY and HENRY E. COLE-
MAN, Guide to bibliographies of theses, United
States and Canada. American library association:
Chicago 1936. pp.48. [350.]
—— Second edition. 1940. pp.54. [400.]*

[CHARLES WARREN, *ed.*], List of publications by
members of certain college-faculties and learned
societies in the United States, 1867–1872. Bureau
of education: Circulars of information (1873,
no.4): Washington 1873. pp.72. [1500.]

R[ICHARD] R[OGERS] BOWKER, *ed.* Publications of
societies. A provisional list of the publications of
american scientific, literary, and other societies
from their organization. New York 1899. pp.v.
181. [7500.]

A LIST of american doctoral dissertations printed
in 1912 [&c.] received in the Catalog division.
Library of Congress: Washington.
    1912. By Charles A[lcott] Flagg. 1913.
        pp.106. [261.]
    1913. By Alida M[iriam] Stephens. 1914.
        pp.133. [281.]

1914. 1915. pp.157. [311.]

1915. 1916. pp.160. [327.]

1916. 1918. pp.206. [408.]

1917. By Katharine Jacobs. 1921. pp.204. [389.]

1918. 1921. pp.200. [373.]

1919. By Mary Wilson MacNair. 1921. pp.167. [268.]

1920. 1922. pp.179. [310.]

1921. 1923. pp.252. [397.]

1922. 1924. pp.238. [490.]

1923. 1925. pp.209. [428.]

1924. 1926. pp.vii.173. [511.]

1925. 1927. pp.vii.206. [614.]

1926. 1928. pp.vii.262. [669.]

1927. 1929. pp.vii.226. [705.]

1928. 1930. pp.vii.250. [743.]

1929. 1931. pp.vii.275. [840.]

1930. 1932. pp.vii.342. [1092.]

1931. 1933. pp.vii.360. [1140.]

1932. 1934. pp.vii.353. [1095.]

1933. 1935. pp.vii.407. [1276.]

1934. 1936. pp.vii.413. [1283.]

1935. By M. W. MacNair and Margaret Neal Karr. 1937. pp.vii.407. [1244.]

1936. 1938. pp.vii.416. [1291.]

1937. 1939. pp.vii.422. [1260.]

1938. 1940. pp.vii.420. [1254.]
no more published.

EVA ALICE COLE, A check list of biographical directories and general catalogues of american colleges. New York 1915. pp.7. [160.]

TITLES of masters' and doctors' theses in education accepted by colleges and universities in the United States. [Urbana] 1917–1927.
details of this work are entered under Academic writings: Education, above.

DOCTORATES conferred in the [arts and] sciences by american universities. 1919 &c.
details of this work are entered under Science: United States, below.

TITLES of completed research from home economics departments in american colleges and universities, 1918 to 1923. Bureau of education: Home economics circular (no.18): Washington [1924]. pp.14. [250.]

R[AY] M[ARCH] MERRILL, American doctoral dissertations in the romance field, 1876–1926. Institut des études françaises: New York 1927. pp.88. [500.]

THESES and dissertations by chinese students in America. China institute in America: Bulletin (no.4): New York [1927]. pp.[ii].42. [568.]

— Supplementary list . . . (no.7): 1928. pp.12. [728.]

— [supplement]. Theses . . . 1931–1936. Compiled by M. Hsitien Lin [Mou-shêng Lin]. China institute in America: [1936]. pp.31. [619.]

R[OY] A[NDREW] SEATON, *ed.* Engineering experiment station record. . . . A summary of engineering research at the land-grant colleges and universities. Association of land-grant colleges and universities: [Lancaster, Pa. 1929]. pp.vii.98. [1263.]

[—] — [another edition]. [Edited by John Hard Lampe]. [1945]. pp.134. [3500.]

A PARTIAL list of titles of essays written by candidates for the master's degree in colleges and universities of the United States, 1929–'30. Fort Hays state college: Current problems in research: Bulletin (no.1 = Fort Hays Kansas state college bulletin, vol.xxi. no.3): Topeka 1931. pp.60. [1512.]

THESES on pan american topics prepared by candidates for degrees in universities and colleges in the United States. Pan american union: Colum-

bus memorial library: Bibliographic series (no.5):
Washington 1931. pp.52. [502.]
— Third edition. 1941. f.[i].4.170.*

A CATALOGUE of publications in the humanities
by american learned societies. American council
of learned societies: Washington 1932. pp.[ii].72.
[300.]

RECENT theses in education . . . deposited with
the Office of education and available for loan.
Office of education: Pamphlet (no.26): Washington 1932. pp.iii.41. [242.]
— [another edition]. Doctors' theses [&c]. By
Ruth A. Gray. . . . (no.60): 1935. pp.[ii].69. [797.]

ANNOTATED list of 800 graduate theses and dissertations in industrial-arts education and vocational-industrial education accepted by institutions
of higher learning in the United States, 1892–1933.
[Iowa state college: Ames 1933]. ff.[xii].89. [800.]*

DISSERTATIONS in american church history
(1889–1932). Catholic university of America:
American church history seminar bulletins (no.1):
Washington 1933. pp.27. [184.]
privately printed.

PRISCILLA HISS and ROBERTA FANSLER, Research
in fine arts in the colleges & universities of the

United States. Carnegie corporation: New York 1934. pp.vii.224. [215.]

FREDERICK EBY and S. E. FROST, Graduate theses and dissertations written in the field of education at Baylor university, Southern methodist university, Texas christian university, Texas technological college, the university of Texas, West Texas state teachers college, the university of Texas, West Texas state teachers college. [Austin 1934]. pp.85. [823.]

DOCTORAL dissertations accepted by american universities. Compiled for the National research council and the American council of learned societies by the Association of research libraries [for the Association of research libraries]. New York.

> i. 1933–1934. Edited by Donald B[ean] Gil-christ. pp.xvii.98. [2620.]
> ii. 1934–1935. pp.xv.102. [2649.]
> iii. 1935–1936. pp.xvii.102. [2683.]
> iv. 1936–1937. pp.xvii.105. [2709.]
> v. 1937–1938. pp.xiv.98. [2768.]
> vi. 1938–1939. pp.xiii.113. [2928.]
> vii. 1939–1940. Edited by Edward A[twood] Henry. pp.xv.126. [3088.]
> viii. 1940–1941. pp.xiv.142. [3526.]

ix. 1941–1942. pp.xvii.128. [3243.]

x. 1942–1943. pp.xvii.110. [2689.]

xi. 1943–1944. pp.[ii].xiii.88. [2117.]

xii. 1944–1945. Edited by Arnold H[erman] Trotier. pp.[ii].xiii.68. [1576.]

xiii. 1945–1946. pp.[ii].xiii.71. [1708.]

xiv. 1946–1947. pp.[ii].xiii.100. [2587.]

xv. 1947–1948. pp.[ii].xiv.137. [3609.]

xvi. 1948–1949. Edited by A. H. Trotier and Marian Harman. pp.xvii.176. [4853.]

xviii. 1949–1950. pp.xvii.235. [6510.]

xviii. 1950–1951. pp.xv.266. [7477.]

xix. 1951–1952. pp.xv.269. [7661.]

xx. 1952–1953. pp.xvi.305. [8604.]

xxi. 1953–1954. pp.xvi.312. [9000.]

xxii. 1954–1955. pp.xvi.298. [8812.]

[*continued as:*]

Index to american doctoral dissertations combined with Dissertation abstracts.*

1955–1956. pp.xiii.171. [8699.]

1956–1957. pp.xv.209. [8363.]

1957–1958. pp.xvii.182. [8799.]

1958–1959. pp.xv.200. [9295.]

1959–1960. pp.xxi.218. [9927.]

1960–1961. pp.xxi.228. [10,343.]

THESES submitted for advanced degrees in the subject matter of forestry, in colleges and universities of the United States. Oregon state college library: [Corvallis] 1938. ff.[i].86. [840.]*

MICROFILM abstracts. A collection of abstracts of doctoral dissertations which are available in complete form on microfilm. Ann Arbor.*

    i. 1938. pp.vii.32. [20.]

    ii. 1939–1940. pp.ix.57+xi.136. [150.]

    iii. 1941. pp.v.54+[ii].ix.119. [100.]

    iv. 1942. pp.vii.71+xi.167. [200.]

    v. 1943–1944. pp.v.81+vi.135. [200.]

    vi. 1945. pp.vii.150+ix.137. [200.]

    vii. 1946–1947. pp.ix.110+[ii].xi.143. [200.]

    viii. 1948. pp.xiii.160+xiii.190. [300.]

    ix. 1949–1950. pp.xv.234+xiii.239+xiii.236. [400.]

    x. 1950. pp.xii. 142+xii.192+xvi.292+xix. 406. [500.]

    xi. 1951. pp.1212. [500.]

    — Microfilm abstracts author index . . . 1938–1951. Special libraries association: Georgia chapter: Atlanta 1956. pp.iv.27.

[continued as:]

Dissertation abstracts. A guide to dissertations and monographs available in microfilm.

    xii. 1952. pp.914. [1250.]

    xiii. 1953. pp.1396. [2000.]

xiv. 1954. pp.2554. [5000.]
xv. 1955. pp.2742. [5000.]
xvi. 1956. pp.2576+xiii.171. [5000.]
xvii. 1957. pp.2107. [4000.]
xviii. 1957–1958. pp.2288+xv.182. [4500.]
xix. 1958–1959. pp.343+xv.200. [6500.]
xx. 1959–1960. pp.4888+xx.218. [9000.]
xxi. 1960–1961. pp.3907+xxi.228. [8000.]
xii. 1961–1962. pp.4464 + 258 + 3465. [9000.]
xxiii. 1962–1963. pp.4806. [9500.]

in progress; from vol.xvi absorbed Doctoral dissertations.

DOCTORAL dissertations on Japan, accepted by american universities, 1912–1939. Japan institute: New York 1940. ff.vii.17. [89.]*

SAMUEL SELDEN, *ed.* Research in drama and the theatre in the universities and colleges of the United States, 1937–1942. A bibliography. American educational theatre association: Meadville, Pa. [1944]. pp.[iv].48. [750.]

LIST of doctoral dissertations in history now in progress at universities in the United States. American historical association: Washington [1949]. pp.55. [1634.]
500 copies printed.

[MARY LOUISE RUKA], The Wisconsin region. A bibliography of theses in the social sciences and humanities. [University of Wisconsin centennial committee: Madison 1949]. ff.[ii].42.12 [*sic*, 14]. [750.]*

T[HOMAS] K[IRK] CURETON, Doctorate theses reported by graduate departments of health, physical education and recreation, 1930–1946, inclusively. [Washington 1949]. pp.[39]. [420.]
limited to United States theses.

THE SOCIOLOGY of the south: a bibliography and critique of unpublished doctoral dissertations and master's theses written on aspects of the south, 1938–1948. Fisk university: Social science institute: Social science source documents (no.6): Nashville 1950. ff.[i].iii.376. [223.]*

INDUSTRIAL relations theses and dissertations submitted at seventeen [thirty-eight] universities. University of California: Institute of industrial relations: Berkeley.*
  1949–1950. Edited by Gwendolyn Lloyd. ff.[i].40. [350.]
  1950–1951.
  1951–1952.
  1952–1953.
  1953–1954. Edited by G. Lloyd and Paul M.

Miles. ff.[i].vii.67. [600.]
1954–1955. ff.[i].vii.40. [473.]
1955–1956. ff.[i].ix.47. [529.]

HANS [THEODORE] DAVID [*and others*], A list of doctoral dissertations in musicology and allied fields. Music teachers national association [&c.]: Denton, Texas 1951. ff.[i].41. [325.]*
limited to the universities of the United States and Canada.

MASTER's theses in education. Cedar Falls, Iowa. 1951 &c.
in progress; details of this work are entered under Education, below.

THOMAS K[IRK] CURETON, Masters theses in health, physical education and recreation. American association for health, physical education and recreation: Washington 1952. pp.iii.292. [3878.]*

JOHN ALAN JONES, List of unpublished doctoral dissertations and masters theses in the field of anthropology bearing on north american Indians north of Mexico. Department of justice: Washington [1952]. ff.19. [225.]*

BIBLIOGRAPHY of studies completed at Utah colleges and universities. Utah educational research bulletin (vol.4, no.1 &c.): [Salt Lake City].

    1952. . . . (vol.4, no.1). pp.[iv].12. [110.]

    1953. . . . (vol.5, no.1). pp.[v].9. [80.]

    1954–1955. . . . (vol.6, no.1). pp.[iii].20. [225.]

    1956.

           [continued as:]

Annotated bibliography of studies in education completed at Utah graduate schools.

    1957. . . . (vol.8, no.1). pp.[iii].19. [100.]

    1958. . . . (vol.9, no.1). pp.[iii].23. [135.]

    1959. . . . (vol.10, no.1). pp.[iv].32. [145.]

    1960. . . . (vol.11, no.1). pp.[iii].40. [190.]

    1961. . . . (vol.12, no.1). pp.[iv].38. [130.]

in progress.

KATHERINE W[HIPPLE] HUGUES, RAY A. YODER and WILLIAM I. WEST, Forestry theses accepted by colleges and universities in the United States 1900-1952. Oregon state college: Bibliographic series (no.3): Corvallis 1953. pp.140. [2638.]

HARRY KANTOR, A bibliography of unpublished doctoral disserations [*sic*] and masters theses dealing with the governments, politics and international relations of latin America. Inter-american bibliographical and library association (1st ser., vol.xiii): Gainesville, Fla. 1953. pp.85.

Academic Writings

TITLES of theses submitted for doctoral degrees in chemistry and chemical engineering at american educational institutions October 1, 1951 to October 30, 1952. American chemical society: Committee on professional training: Washington [1953]. pp.[iv].55. [600.]

FACULTIES, publications and doctoral theses in chemistry and chemical engineering at United States universities. American chemical society: Committee on professional training: [Washington] 1953 &c.*

details of this work are entered under Academies: Chemistry, above.

MARY LOUISE LYDA and STANLEY B[ARBER] BROWN, Research studies in education. A subject index of doctoral dissertations, reports, and field studies. Boulder, Colo. 1953 &c.*

in progress.

SURVEY of research investigations in progress and contemplated in the field of latin american subjects in colleges and universities in the United States and Canada. Gainesville 1953 &c.

in progress; details of this work are entered under America, below.

BARTON BLEDSOE, Masters' theses in science,

1952. Washington [1954]. pp.252. [5588.]

ELIZABETH WIEGAND, Selected bibliography of theses and research in family economics, home management and related areas. American home economics association: Washington 1954. pp.16. [225.]*

—— Supplement . . . by Emma G. Holmes. 1957. pp.19. [250.]*

[DANIEL S. TURNER], Bibliography of geology theses, colleges and universities of the United States. Denver [1954]. pp.[iii].483. [5750.]*

[—] — [another edition]. Bibliography of theses written for advanced degrees in geology and related sciences at universities and colleges in the United States and Canada through 1957. By [Byron] John Chronic and Halka Chronic. 1958. pp.[428]. [11,091.]*

CLYDE H[ULL] CANTRELL and WALTON R. PATRICK, Southern literary culture. A bibliography of masters' and doctors' theses. [University, Ala. 1955]. pp.xiv.124. [2529.]*

NED ROSEN and RALPH E[DWARD] MAC COY, Doctoral dissertations in labor and industrial relations, 1933–1953. University of Illinois: Institute of labor and industrial relations: Bibliographic contribution (no.5): Champaign 1955. ff.iv.86. [1031.]*

CLAUDE ELLIOTT, Theses on Texas history . . . produced in the department of history of eighteen Texas graduate schools and thirty-three graduate schools outside of Texas, 1907–1952. Texas state historical association: Austin 1955. pp.xi.280. [652.]

JAMES TAYLOR DUNN, Master's theses and doctoral dissertations on New York history, 1870–1954. (Revised). [*s. l.*] 1955. pp.20. [400.]

WALTER CROSBY EELLS, American doctoral dissertations on education in countries of the middle east. Middle east institute: Washington 1955. ff.28. [200.]*

DISSERTATIONS and theses relating to personnel administration accepted by american colleges and universities. Civil service commission: Library: Washington.*
    1955. pp.20. [200.]
    1956. pp.[ii].23. [250.]

MARY E[LIZABETH] MORRIS, Bibliography of theses on Oklahoma in the university of Oklahoma library. University of Oklahoma: Institute of community development: Norman 1956. ff.[i].ii.104. [1250.]*

FREDERICK J. DOCKSTADER, The american Indian in graduate studies. A bibliography of theses and dissertations. Museum of the american Indian: Contributions (vol.xv): New York 1957. pp.xvii. 399. [3684.]

CUMULATIVE catalogue of theses 1937–1956. American bankers association: Graduate school of banking: New York [1957]. pp.199.

BIBLIOGRAPHY of graduate theses in the field of marketing written at U.S. colleges and universities 1950–1957. New York university: Graduate school of business administration: [New York 1957]. ff.[ii].92. [1400.]*

FERN L. WILSON, Wilson's index of publications by university bureaus of business research. [Cleveland 1957]. pp.303. [2500.]*
— — Supplement. 1957. ff.118. [1000.]*

JAMES [LESLIE] WOODRESS, Dissertations in american literature 1891–1955. Durham, N. C. 1957. pp.x.100. [2500.]
— — 1891–1961. 1962. pp.xii.138. [3000.]

GEORGE E. TARBOX, Bibliography of graduate

theses on geophysics in U. S. and canadian institutions. Colorado school of mines: Quarterly (vol.53, no.1): Golden 1958. pp.vi.55. [450.]★

ROBERT M. JENKINS, *ed.* Bibliography of theses on fishery biology . . . and related subjects. Sport fishing institute: [Washington] 1959. pp.[iii].80. [1743.]★

HOMER E[DWARD] SOCOLOFSKY, Kansas history in graduate study. A bibliography of theses and dissertations. Kansas state university of agriculture and applied science: Manhattan 1959. pp.64. [942.]

MARTIN J. BUSS, Old testament dissertations 1928–1958. [Ann Arbor 1959]. pp.x.57.

JOHN CHAVIS, A brief survey of theses in Michigan history. [Detroit 1959]. ff.ii.pp.20. [300.]★

LAWRENCE C[ALVIN] LITTLE, Bibliography of doctoral dissertations in character and religious education. University of Pittsburgh: Department of religious education: Pittsburgh [1960]. pp. [iii].273. [5000.]★

JESSE J[OHN] DOSSICK, Doctoral research on Russia and the Soviet Union. [New York] 1960. pp.[vii].248. [2000.]

RICHARD D[ANIEL] ALTICK and WILLIAM R. MAT-
THEWS,Guide to doctoral dissertations in victorian
literature 1886–1958. Urbana 1960. pp.vii.119.
[2105.]*

FRANKLN PARKER, Negro education in the
U.S.A.; a bibliography of doctoral dissertations.
Austin 1960. ff.9. [100.]*

LIST of publications. American universities field
staff: New York.*
    i. [1951]–1959. [1960]. pp.xi.71. [900.]
in progress.

M. LOIS MARCKWORTH, Dissertations in physics.
An indexed bibliography of all doctoral theses
accepted by american universities, 1861–1959.
Stanford 1961. pp.xii.803. [8418.]*

T'UNG-LI YÜAN, A guide to doctoral dissertations
by chinese students in America 1905–1960. Sino-
american culture society: Washington 1961. pp.iii–
xix.248. [2779.]*

FRANKLIN H[AYWARD] KNOWER, Bibliography
of communications dissertations in american
schools of theology. [s. l. 1961]. ff.45. [863.]*

FRANKLN PARKER Audio-visual education; a

bibliography of doctoral dissertations. Austin [1961]. ff.17. [209.]*

FRANKLIN PARKER, The american high school; a bibliography of . . . doctoral dissertations. Austin [1961]. ff.9. [131.]*

FRANKLIN PARKER, Biographies of educators; a partial list of american doctoral dissertations. Austin [1961]. pp.8. [120.]*

FRANKLIN PARKER, Canadian education; bibliography of doctoral dissertations. Austin [1961]. ff.9. [131.]*

FRANKLIN PARKER, Catholic education: a partial list of american doctoral dissertations. Austin 1961. ff.12. [189.]*

FRANKLIN PARKER, Fifty years of the junior high school; . . . a bibliography of . . . doctoral dissertations. Austin [1961]. pp.15. [131.]*

FRANKLIN PARKER, Jewish education: a partial list of american doctoral dissertations. Austin 1961. ff.5. [60.]*

FRANKLIN PARKER, School desegregation; a list of doctoral dissertations. [Austin 1961]. pp.[8]. [94.]*

FRANKLIN PARKER, Teacher education; a biblio-

graphy of . . . doctoral dissertations. Austin [1961].
pp.32. [705.]★

STELLA TRAWEEK, A survey of university business and economic research reports . . . 1957
through 1961. Small business administration:
Washington [1961]. pp.xii.642. [2298.]★

[—] — [another edition]. A survey . . . 1957
through 1963. Prepared by Cynthia R. Bettinger,
Charles T. Clark. 1963. pp.xiii.690. [3623.]★

FRANKLIN PARKER, The community junior college . . .; a bibliography of . . . doctoral research
dissertations. Austin [1961]. pp.16. [188.]★
— — [supplement]. [1961]. pp.4. [38.]★

LAWRENCE C[ALVIN] LITTLE, Researches in per-
sonality, character and religious education. A
bibliography of american doctoral dissertations
1885 to 1959. [Pittsburgh] 1962. pp.iv.215.
[6304.]★

A LIST of american doctoral dissertations on
Africa. Library of Congress: General reference and
bibliography division: Washington 1962. pp.[v].
69. [700.]

VINCENT LANIER, Doctoral research in art education. [Los Angeles] 1962. pp.[ii].52.[xx]. [450.]★

Academic Writings

LAWRENCE C[ALVIN] LITTLE, A bibliography of doctoral dissertations on adults and adult education. University of Pittsburgh: Department of religious education: Pittsburgh 1962. pp.[iii].82. [1000.]*

—— Revised edition. 1963. pp.iv.163. [2500.]*

BETTY [MARGARET ELIZABETH] VAN DER SMISSEN, A bibliography of research theses and dissertations only related to recreation. State university of Iowa: Iowa City 1962. pp.[ii].ii.119. [961.]*

ELTON F. HENLEY, A check list of masters' theses in the United States on William Wordsworth. University of Virginia: Bibliographical society: [Charlottesville 1962]. pp.ii.29.[xi]. [381.]*

KENNETH R. SPARKS, A bibliography of doctoral dissertations in television and radio. Syracuse university: School of journalism: Syracuse, N.Y. [1962]. ff.[iii].32. [352.]*

MASTERS abstracts. Abstracts of selected masters theses on microfilm. Ann Arbor.*
    i. 1962. pp.viii.49+viii.64. [500.]
    ii. 1964. pp.vii.22+
in progress.

CURTIS W. STUCKI, American doctoral dissertations on Asia, 1933–1962, including appendix of masters's theses at Cornell university. Cornell university: Southeast Asia program: Data paper (no.50): Ithaca, N.Y. 1963. pp.204.

FRANKLIN PARKER, Latin american education research. An annotated bibliography of... United States doctoral dissertation. University of Texas: Institute of latin american studies: Austin [1963]. pp.63. [269.]*

LEO C. FAY, WELDON G. BRADTMUELLER and EDWARD G. SUMMERS, Doctoral studies in reading, 1919 through 1960. Indiana university: School of education: Bulletin (vol.40, no.4): [Bloomington] 1964. pp.vi.80.*

Uzbekistan

УКАЗАТЕЛЬ докторских и кандидатских диссертаций защищенных в Узбекистане в 1936–1951 гг. Общественные науки, естественные науки, математика. Среднеазиатский государственный университет им. Ленина [&c.]: Материалы к библиографии (vol.iv): Ташкент 1954. pp.175. [595.]

Aberdeen, university of.

[PETER JOHN ANDERSON], Marischal college and university, Aberdeen, 1593–1860. Collections towards the preparation of the fasti. [Aberdeen 1886]. pp.28. [large number.]
112 copies privately printed.

P[ETER] J[OHN] ANDERSON, Collections towards a bibliography of the universities of Aberdeen Edinburgh bibliographical society: Publications (vol.viii): Edinburgh 1907. pp.viii.160. [1250.]
82 copies printed.

J[AMES] F[OWLER] KELLAS JOHNSTONE, The lost Aberdeen theses. Aberdeen 1916. pp.23. [300.]

ABSTRACTS of theses accepted by the university for higher degrees. University: Aberdeen.
    1931–1932. pp.23. [15.]
    1932–1933. pp.31. [20.]
    1933–1934. pp.42. [30.]
    1934–1935. pp.23. [15.]
    1935–1936. pp.32. [20.]
    1936–1937. pp.24. [15.]
no more published.

Acadia university.

HAZEL G. MORSE, Acadia authors: a bibliography.
Acadia bulletin (vol.xi, no.11): Wolfville, N.S.
1922. pp.44. [1000.]

Adelaide, university of.

RESEARCH. Report on work carried out.
[Adelaide].*

    1952. pp.124. [750.]
    1953. pp.166. [1000.]
    1954. pp.185. [1000.]
    1955. pp.212. [1000.]
    1956. pp.226. [1000.]
    1957. pp.250. [1000.]
    1958. pp.250. [1000.]
    1959. pp.296. [1000.]
    1960. pp.352. [1000.]
    1961. pp.432. [1000.]
  in progress.

Agricultural and mechanical college of Texas.

FACULTY publications. [College Station].
    1957–1961. 1963. pp.128. [2000.]
  in progress.

Air university.

AIR university annotated list of student research reports. Maxwell air force base, Ala.★

    i. 1957. pp.iv.91. [204.]

    ii. 1958. pp.iv.168. [321.]

    iii. 1959. pp.iv.146. [282.]

    iv. 1960. [By V. Estelle Phillips]. pp.iv.102. [194.]

    v. 1961. pp.iv.144. [272.]

    vi. 1962. pp.iv.213. [429.]

    vii. 1963. pp.iv.228. [467.]

 in progress.

Alabama, university of.

BIBLIOGRAPHY of master's theses, university of Alabama, 1925–1937. University of Alabama: Bulletin (new ser., no.161): [University] 1937. pp.32. [600.]

— 1900–1952. By Catherine T. Jones [*and others*]. . . . (vol.51, no.9): 1957. pp.146. [2111.]

PUBLICATIONS and thesis direction [Publications] at the university of Alabama. University of Alabama: Bulletin (vol. , no. &c.): University

    1947–1948. pp.[vi].30. [208.]

    1948–1949. pp.[vi].34. [332.]

1949–1950. . . . (vol.44, no.13). pp.[v].62. [537.]

1950–1951. . . . (vol.45, no.11). pp.[v].49. [616.]

1951–1952. . . . (vol.46, no.21). pp.[vii]. 56. [552.]

1952–1953. . . . (vol.47, no.   ).

1953–1954. . . . (vol.48, no.   ).

1954–1955. . . . (vol.49, no.   ).

1955–1956. . . . vol.50, no.15). pp.[vii].54. [614.]

1956–1957. . . . vol.51, no.16). pp.v.61. [740.]

1957–1958. . . . (vol.52, no.17). pp.[v].55. [645.]

1958–1959. . . . (vol.53, no.14). pp.[v].56. [648.]

in progress?

CURRENT research of the faculty and staff of the university of Alabama. University of Alabama: Bulletin (vol.44, no.3 &c.): University.

1949–1950. . . . (vol.44, no.3). pp.[iii].32. [367.]

Altdorf, university of.

GUSTAV GEORG ZELTNER, Vitae theologorvm altorphinorvm a condita academia omnivm vna cum scriptorvm recensv plenivs et accvrativs.

Norimbergæ &c. 1772. pp.[viii].511.[xxiv]. [1500.]

SIGMUND JACOB APIN, Vitae professorvm philosophiae qvi a condita academia altorfina ad hvnc vsqve diem clarvervnt. Norimbergæ &c. 1728. pp.[xvi.]346.[vi.] [1000.]

a copy in the British museum contains ms. notes and corrections.

JO[HANN] JAC[OB] BAIER, Biographiae professorvm medicinae qvi in academia altorfina vnqvam vixervnt. Norimbergæ &c. 1728. pp.[x].195.[v]. [500.]

American university of Beirut.

LIST of publications of the Faculty of arts and sciences of the American university of Beirut. American university of Beirut: Publications: Social science series (no.4 = Minor studies, 1942, A): [Beirut] 1942. pp.[ii].15. [300.]

Andhra university.

RESEARCH work of the university teachers. [Madras 1946]. pp.75. [1250.]
— Supplement. Choolai 1949. pp.43. [750.]

Ankara, university of.

ANKARA üniversitesi fen fakültesi yayınları kataloğu. İstanbul 1952. pp.[iv].31. [100.]

TÜRKER ACAROGLU, Üniversitesi yayımları bibliyografyası, 1926–1951. Ankara 1952 &c.
in progress.

ANKARA üniversitesi tip fakültesi öğretim üyelerinin kitap yayınları. Ankara 1960. pp.16. [125.]
the copy in the Library of Congress contains ms. additions and corrections.

Annamalai university.

RESEARCH in the Annamalai university. [Chidambaram] 1955. pp.36. [50.]

Arizona, university of.

ABSTRACTS of theses for higher degrees. University of Arizona: Record (vol.xxviii, no.1 [&c.]): Tucson.

1934 ... (vol.xxviii, no.1): 1935. pp.36. [50.]

1935–1936 ... (vol.xxx, no.1): 1937. pp.62. [125.]

1937–1938 ... (vol.xxxii, no.1): 1939. pp.75. [150.]

1939–1940 . . . (vol.xxxiv, no.1): 1941. pp.81. [150.]

1941–1942 . . . (vol. , no.1): 1943. pp.

1943–1944 . . . (vol.xxxviii, no.1): 1945. pp.34. [50.]

1945–1946 . . . (vol.xl, no.1): 1947. pp.36. [50.]

[*continued as:*]

Check list of theses accepted for masters' and doctors' degrees.★

[*continued as:*]

Checklist of theses accepted for higher degrees.★

1947–1951. Compiled by Donald M. Powell. ff.[ii].20. [400.]

1952–1956. ff.[i].20. [400.]

1957–1961. ff.[ii].34. [600.]

in progress; only the cumulated editions have been recorded.

Arkansas, university of.

FACULTY and staff publications, 1952–1957. [Fayetteville 1957]. ff.viii.212. [2500.]★

Atlanta university.

GRADUATE theses of Atlanta university. Atlanta university: Library: Atlanta, Ga.

i. 1931–1942. By Gaynelle [Wright] Barksdale. 1944. pp.71. [402.]

ii. 1943–1947. pp.58. [392.]

iii. 1948–1953. Compiled by G. W. Barksdale and Edward B. Miller. pp.102. [780.]

Auburn university.

PUBLICATIONS by members of the staff. Alabama polytechnic institute.

 1945.
 1946. ff.[iii].16. [125.]★
   [*continued as:*]
Faculty publications.
 1947–1953. By Robert R[ight] Rea. pp.63. [1750.]

Australian national university.

CHECK list of current and forthcoming publications. [Canberra] 1960. pp.14.

Baylor university.

FREDERICK EBY and S. E. FROST, Graduate theses and dissertations written in the field of education at Baylor university, Southern methodist university, Texas christian university. Texas technological college, the university of Texas, West Texas state teachers college, the university of Texas, West Texas state teachers college. [Austin 1934]. pp.85. [823.]

Beirut, university of.

BIBLIOGRAPHIE de l'Université Saint-Joseph de Beyrouth. Beyrouth 1951. pp.207. [1500.]

Belgrade, university of.

докторске дисертације на Београдском университету, 1905-1950. Београдски университет: Београд 1951. pp.21. [254.]

Berlin, university of.

[WILHELM ERMAN], Verzeichnis der Berliner universitätsschriften 1810-1885. Nebst einem anhang enthaltend die ausserordentlichen und ehrenpromotionen. Berlin 1899. pp.xi.848. [9697.]

WILHELM SCHONACK, Ein jahrhundert berliner philologischer dissertationen (1810-1910). Wolfenbüttel 1914. pp.x.232. [1500.]

Bogotà, university of.

ANGELA HERNÁNDEZ-ARANGO and LUCÍA VALENCIA M., Tesis de grado presentadas a la Facultad

nacional de agronomía de Medellín. Medellín
1954. ff.[i].27. [246.]★

Bologna, university of.

CATALOGO dei lavori pubblicati dai professori,
dai dottori collegiati e dagli assistenti nella R. uni-
versitá di Bologna. Bologna 1875. pp.96. [1000.]

CARLO MALAGOLA, I libri della nazione tedesca
presso lo studio bolognese. Note storico-biblio-
grafiche. Modena 1884. pp.[iii].59. [58.]

Bonn, university of.

FRITZ MILKAU, Verzeichniss der bonner universitätsschriften 1818–1885. Nebst einem Anhang
enthaltend die ausserordentlichen promotionen.
Bonn 1897. pp.xxiv.441. [3250.]

BONNER literatur-kalender. Bonn 1949.
— [another edition]. 1961. pp.[viii].146. [1500.]

JAHRBUCH der dissertationen. Rheinische Friedrich-Wilhelms-universität Bonn: Medizinische
fakultät: Bonn.

    i. 1951. pp.261. [250.]
    ii. 1952. pp.171. [250.]
    iii. 1952–1953. pp.223. [250.]

iv. 1953–1954. pp.230. [250.]
v. 1954–1955. pp.187. [200.]
vi. 1955–1956. pp.181. [200.]
vii. 1956–1957. pp.157. [150.]
viii. 1957–1959. pp.191. [200.]
in progress.

Breslau, university of.

KARL PRETZCH, Verzeichnis der breslauer universitätsschriften, 1811–1885. Breslau 1905. pp. xv.387. [3079.]

FELIX HAASE, Die schriftstellerische tätigkeit der breslauer theologischen fakultäten von 1811 bis 1911. Festschrift zur hundertjahrfeier der universität: Breslau 1911. pp.vii.306. [1500.]

ALEKSANDER ROMBOWSKI, Materiały bibliograficzne do pięciolecia uniwersytetu i politechniki we Wrocławiu, 1945–1950. Uniwersytet: Biblioteka: Informator (vol.xiii): Wrocław 1950. pp. [iv].61. [730.]*

Brigham Young university.

BIBLIOGRAPHY of masters' theses . . . submitted to the graduate school. Brigham Young university: Bulletin (vol.liii, no.6): Provo [1956]. pp.96. [900.]

THESES, dissertations, and publications of the faculty. Brigham Young university: Bulletin [vol. 53, no.23): Provo [1956]. pp.102. [1750.]

Bristol, university of.

JUBILEE research survey. A survey of recent research. [Bristol] 1959. pp.v.151. [1500.]

Brown university.

GEORGE PARKER WINSHIP, Brown university broadsides. Providence 1913. pp.[7]. [12.]
200 copies printed.

GEORGE K. ANDERSON, Books and articles by members of the department: a bibliography. Brown university: English department: Providence 1961. pp.40. [750.]

Buenos Aires, university of.

MARCIAL R. CANDIOTI, Bibliografía doctoral de la universidad de Buenos Aires y catálogo cronológico de las tesis en su primer centenario. Buenos Aires 1920. pp.804. [8500.]
500 copies printed.

TESIS doctorales de la Facultad de ciencias económicas, 1916–1951. Catálogo. Universidad nacional: Buenos Aires 1952. pp.83. [543.]

Calcutta, university of.

DESCRIPTIVE catalogue of university publications. University of Calcutta: Calcutta.

 1930. pp.[ii].92.7. [500.]
 1931. pp.[ii].177. [600.]
 1932. pp.[ii].133. [750.]

California, university of.

CATALOGUE. University of California press publications, 1893–1943. Berkeley &c. 1944. pp.ix. 258. [4200.]

[AURA D. HARDISON], Record of theses submitted in partial fulfillment of the requirements for the degree of doctor of philosophy at the university of California, 1885–1926. [Berkeley] 1926. pp.[ii]. 132. [483.]★

supplements have been issued.

J[OE] W[ILLIAM] JOHNSON, Theses and reports on fluid mechanics and related fields (1900–1945) and publications of Fluid mechanics laboratory (1926–1945). University of California: Department of engineering: Berkeley 1945. ff.[i].35. [343.]★

EMILY C. LUMBARD, Engineering, economic, social and legal aspects of water. Theses presented for higher degrees, University of California . . . 1900–1957. University of California: Water resources center archives: Report (no.2): Berkeley 1958. pp.[ii].73. [439.]*

RESEARCH directory. A compilation of research projects. University of California: Los Angeles 1958 &c.

in progress.

GERALD J. GIEFER and CYNTHIA BARNES, Bachelor of science theses on water resources engineering, university of California, Berkeley. University of California: Water resources center archives: Report (no.6): Berkeley 1959. pp.[iii].93. [598.]*

Cambridge, university of.

ABSTRACTS of dissertations approved for the ph.d., m.sc., and m.litt. degrees in the university of Cambridge during the academical year. Cambridge.

1940–1941. pp.120. [69.]
1941–1942. pp.72. [39.]
1942–1943. pp.40. [22.]
1943–1944. pp.46. [25.]

1944–1945. pp.53. [25.]
1945–1946. pp.58. [32.]
1946–1947. pp.66. [38.]
1947–1948. pp.132. [83.]
1948–1949. pp.197. [147.]
1949–1950. pp.248. [173.]
1950–1951. pp.228. [179.]
1951–1952. pp.xvii.243. [200.]
1952–1953. pp.xviii.272. [250.]
1953–1954. pp.xvii.283. [250.]
1954–1955. pp.xviii.261. [250.]
1955–1956. pp.xvii.268. [250.]
1956–1957. pp.xviii.267. [250.]
　　　　　[continued as:]
Titles of dissertations [&c.].
1957–1958. pp.[iii].25. [275.]
1958–1959. pp.[v].21. [225.]
1959–1960. pp.[v].20. [200.]
1960–1961. pp.
1961–1962. pp.[v].27. [300.]
in progress.

Capetown, university of.

REPORT on publications and research [Research and publications] in the university. [Capetown].
1947–1949. pp.[viii].88. [250.]
1950–1952.

1953–1955. pp.[vi].104. [300.]
1956–1958. pp.[iii].69. [1000.]
in progress.

Cervera, university of.

CATÁLOGO de la exposición de conclusiones académicas de la universidad de Cervera impresas en la ciudad. Instituto de estudios ilerdenses: Lérida.
[i]. 1943. pp.39.
ii. 1944. pp.22. [37.]
iii. 1945. pp.21. [54.]
iv. 1946. pp.22. [59.]

Chicago, university of.

THE REPORT of the president: publications of the members of the university. University of Chicago: Decennial publications (1st ser., vol.ii): Chicago 1904. pp.[xi].185. [6000.]

A RECORD of the doctors in botany of the university of Chicago, 1897–1916. Chicago 1916. ff.vii.82. [500.]

PUBLICATION of the members of the university, 1902–1916. University of Chicago: Chicago 1917. pp.x.518. [7500.]

REGISTER of doctors of philosophy of the university of Chicago, June 1893–June 1927. University of Chicago: Announcements (vol.xxviii, no.4): 1927. pp.138. [2055.]

— [another edition]. Register number, doctors of philosophy, June, 1893–April, 1931. . . . (vol. xxxi, no.19): 1931. pp.iv.174. [2679.]

[CHARLES HUBBARD JUDD], Annotated list of graduate theses and dissertations, the Department of education, the university of Chicago, 1900–1931. Chicago [1932]. pp.[vi].119. [1235.]*

TITLES of graduate theses and dissertations, the Department of education, the university of Chicago, 1932–1935 [&c.]. Chicago 1936 &c.*

THE UNIVERSITY of Chicago press. Catalogue of books and journals, 1891–1941. Chicago 1941. pp.xxxi.432. [2750.]

DOROTHY CHARLES, Dissertations, theses, and papers of the Graduate library school, university of Chicago, 1930–1945. A bibliography. [Chicago 1945]. ff.[ii].28.[iv]. [132.]*

THE UNIVERSITY of Chicago doctoral dissertations and masters' theses on Asia, 1894–1962. University of Chicago: Library: Far eastern library: Chicago [1962]. pp.[ii].iv.52. [630.]*

Chile, universidad de.

ANNUARIO bibliográfico. Universidad: Facultad de filosofía y educación: Santiago.*
> i. 1960. Director: Alberto Villalon Galdames. 1962. pp.3–73. [231.]
> ii. 1961. 1963. pp.3–96. [299.]
in progress.

Cincinnati, university of.

BIBLIOGRAPHICAL record. The graduate school 1900–1910. University of Cincinnati: Record (1st ser., vol.vii, no.2): Cincinnati 1910. pp.36. [500.]

Clark university.

LOUIS N. WILSON, List of degrees granted at Clark university and Clark college. Clark university: Library: Publications (vol.ii, no.9): Worcester, Mass. 1911. pp.39. [274.]
> —— 1889–1914 ... (vol.iv, no.1): 1914. pp.52. [374.]
> —— 1889–1920 ... (vol.vi, no.3): 1920. pp.[ii]. 76. [571.]
mainly a list of theses.

LOUIS N. WILSON, List of papers in the field of religious psychology presented at Clark university. Clark university: Library: Publications (vol. ii, no.8): Worcester, Mass. 1911. pp.9. [122.]

REPORT on research work, with selected bibliographies, of the faculty of Clark university. Clark university: Library: Publications [vol.viii, no.3]: Worcester, Mass. [1932]. pp.[vi].92. [1000.]

DISSERTATIONS and theses. Clark university: Bulletin (no.211 &c.): Worcester, Mass.
    i. 1953. . . . (no.211). pp.[ii].29. [60.] ·
    ii. 1954. . . . (no.214). pp.[ii].24. [50.]
    iii. 1955. . . . (no.219). pp.[ii].25. [50.]
    iv. 1956. . . . (no.224). pp.30. [50.]
    v. 1957. . . . (no.229). pp.37. [50.]
    vi. 1958. . . . (no.232). pp.28. [50.]
    vii. 1959. . . . (no.341). pp.32. [60.]
    viii. 1960. . . . (no.250). pp.28. [50.]
    ix. 1961. . . . (no.258). pp.29. [50.]
    x. 1962. . . . (no.266). pp.27. [50.]
in progress.

Coimbra, university of.

ANTONIO MARIA SEABRA D'ALBUQUERQUE, Bibliographia da imprensa da universidade de

Coimbra nos annos de 1872 a 1873. Coimbra 1874. pp.viii.118. [145.]

—— 1874–1875. 1876. pp.152. [153.]

Colorado, university of.

C[HARLES] HENRY SMITH, Writings and addresses by officers of the university of Colorado, 1877–1913. University of Colorado: Bulletin (vol.xiv, no.4): Boulder 1914. pp.141. [2750.]

Columbia university.

CHARLES ALEXANDER NELSON, Columbiana. A bibliography of manuscripts, pamphlets and books relating to the history of King's college, Columbia college, Columbia university. Columbia university: [New York] 1904. pp.48. [1250.]

[ALICE L. MILLER], List of theses submitted by candidates for the degree of doctor of philosophy . . . 1872–1910. Columbia university: Bulletin of information (10th ser., no.26): New York 1910. pp.[ii].51. [654.]

A BIBLIOGRAPHY of the Faculty of political science of Columbia university, 1880–1930. New York 1931. pp.xi.367. [5000.]

MASTERS essays. Columbia university: New York.

1891–1917. pp.347. [3500.]
1918. pp.28. [250.]

1919. pp.27. [250.]
1920. pp.36. [350.]
1921. pp.40. [350.]
1922. pp.39. [350.]
[*continued as:*]
Essays for the master's degree.
1923. pp.50. [500.]
1924. pp.52. [500.]
[*continued as:*]
Masters essays.
1925. [By Mary Leslie Irwin]. pp.52. [500.]
1926. pp.55. [500.]
1927. [By Margaret Roys]. pp.58. [600.]
1928. pp.68. [700.]
1929. pp.71. [750.]
1930. pp.76. [750.]
1931. pp.71. [750.]
1932. pp.70. [750.]
1933. pp.72. [750.]
1934. [By Therese Siegel]. pp.42. [600.]
1935. pp.39. [600.]
1936. pp.47. [700.]
1937. pp.43. [475.]
1938. pp.49. [500.]

1939. pp.53. [525.]

1940.

1941. pp.47. [500.]

1942.

1943. pp.30. [300.]

1944–1946. [By Rodman Bassein]. pp.29.
[800.]

1947–1949. [By Alice R. Marting]. pp.81.
[1400.]★

1950–1951. [By Alice T. Jacobson]. pp.[iv].
30. [831.]★

1951–1952. pp.[iv].25. [630.]★

absorbed Doctoral dissertations *and continued as:*
Master's essays & doctoral dissertations.

1952–1953. pp.[vi].49. [1185.]★

1953–1954. [By Doris D. Ray]. pp.[viii].35.
[840.]★

1954–1955. pp.[vi].31. [739.]

1955–1956. pp.[vi].30. [707.]★

1956–1957. [By Betty Anne Mayer]. pp.[vi].
30. [738.]★

1957–1958. [By Winnifred Balch (Chiarella)].
pp.[vii].36. [799.]★

1958–1959. [By Winnifred Chiarella]. pp.
[vi].34. [750.]★

in progress?

UNIVERSITY bibliography. Columbia university:

New York.

1909. [By Alice L. Miller]. pp.[ii].35. [750.]
1911 [*sic*, 1910]. [By Isadore Gilbert Mudge].
  pp.[ii].37. [750.]

1911. pp.[ii].iii.60. [1362.]
1912. [By Ethel Richmond]. pp.[ii].iii.64.
  [1406.]
1913. [By Bessie B. Scripture]. pp.[ii].iii.48.
  [1077.]
1914. pp.[ii].52. [1012.]
1915. pp.[v].54. [1052.]
1916. pp.[ii].79. [1462.]
1917. pp.[ii].66. [1232.]
1918. pp.[ii].62. [1162.]
1919. pp.[ii].59. [957.]
1920. pp.[ii].66. [1258.]
1921. pp.[ii].74. [1470.]
1922. pp.85. [1576.]
1923. pp.95. [1706.]
1924. pp.109. [2018.]
1925. pp.101. [1904.]
1926. pp.122. [2311.]
1927. pp.124. [2255.]
1928. pp.125. [2319.]
1929. pp.110. [2067.]
1930. pp.124. [2264.]
1931. pp.[ii].141. [2500.]

no more published; earlier issues formed part of the Columbia university quarterly.

REGISTER of Teachers college doctors of philosophy, 1899–1928[–1934]. Columbia university: New York 1928–1934.

REGISTER of doctoral dissertations accepted in partial fulfillment of the requirements for the degree of doctor of philosophy. Columbia university: Teachers college: New York.

> i. 1899–1936. Edited by Anvor Barstad, Ruth Moses and Eleanor M[ontgomery] Witmer. 1937. [1072.]

REPORTS in industrial engineering. A cumulative bibliography of ph. d. dissertations, masters' reports and selected course papers. Columbia university: Department of industrial [and management] engineering: New York 1949. ff.[iii].61. [1250.]*

— Second edition. 1950. ff.[ii].85. [1750.]*
— — Supplement.*

    1950–1951. ff.[i].9. [125.]
    1951–1952. ff.[i].6. [100.]

Copenhagen, university of.

[SVEND DAHL], Danish theses for the doctorate and commemorative publications of the university of Copenhagen, 1836–1926. A bio–bibliography. Copenhagen &c. 1929. pp.xvi.395. [1250.]

Costa Rica, university of.

LISTA de tesis de grado presentadas a la universidad de Costa Rica hasta 1957. Universidad de

Costa Rica: Publicaciones: Serie bibliotecología (no.10): [San José] 1961. pp.3–381. [2649.]*
— [supplement].
    1958. pp.87. [81.]*

Dartmouth college.

JAMES THAYER GEROULD, Bibliography of Dartmouth college and Hanover. N.H. Concord 1894. pp.60. [750.]

Delft, Technische hogeschool.

[P. J. WILLEKES MACDONALD], Bibliografie der dissertaties ter verkrijging van de titel van doctor in de technische wetenschap en lijst der promoties honoris causa 1905–1955. Technische hogeschool te Delft: 's-Gravenhage 1955. pp.vii.167. [464.]

BIBLIOGRAFIE der dissertaties ter verkrijging van de titel van doctor in de technische wetenschap en lijst der promoties honoris causa, 1905–1955. Technische hogeschool te Delft: 's-Gravenhage 1955. pp.vii.167. [464.]

PUBLICATIONS of the university and doctoral dissertations for the academic year.

    1958–1959. pp.55. [350.]
    1959–1960.
    1960–1961. pp.59. [400.]
    1961–1962. pp.59. [400.]
    1962–1963. pp.58. [400.]
  in progress.

Dorpat, university of.

ABRAHAM GRÜNFELD, Verzeichniss der von der medicinischen facultät zu Dorpat seit ihrer gründung veröffentlichten schriften. Kaiserliche universität Dorpat: Pharmakologisches institut: Historische studien (vol.iii): Halle a. S. 1893. pp.135. [3000.]

Durham, university of.

ABSTRACTS of theses for doctorates presented by candidates who have received the degrees in convocation. University of Durham.

1931–1932. pp.12. [8.]
1932–1933. pp.16. [8.]
1933–1934. pp.12. [8.]
1934–1935. pp.17. [11.]
1935–1936. pp.17. [11.]
1936–1937. pp.17. [11.]
1937–1938. pp.16. [14.]
1938–1939. pp.22. [15.]

East Texas state college.

PUBLICATIONS of the faculty of East Texas state teachers college. Commerce 1942. ff.[i].18. [200.]*

Edinburgh college of art.

ANDREW GRANT bequest. Abstracts of theses presented by Andrew Grant fellows and travelling scholars. Edinburgh college of art: [Edinburgh].

i. 1932–1942. [By M. J. C. Reid]. pp.11. [21.] *in progress.*

Edinburgh university.

STATUTA solennia de doctoratus in medicina gradu in Academia edinburgena capessendo, a facultate medica proposita, et in posterum, jubente senata academico, observanda. [Edinburgh *c.*1800]. pp.36.

LIST of the graduates in medicine in the university of Edinburgh, from M DCCV. to M DCCCLXVI. Edinburgh 1867. pp.vi.187.73. [6000.]
theses are recorded only from 1726.

LIST of theses accepted for doctorates in the academical year 1930–1931 [&c.].

Eidgenössische technische hochschule.

W[ALTER] MIKULASCHEK, Die dissertationen der Eidgenössischen technischen hochschule, 1909–1946. Eine systematische bibliographie. Eidgenössische technische hochschule: Schriftenreihe der bibliothek (no.1): Zürich 1948. pp.142. [1458.]
— — Fortsetzung 1947–1956.... (no.3): [1957]. pp.91. [250.]

Evora, university of.

[ARMANDO NOBRE DE GUSMÃO], IV centenário da fundação da universidade de Évora 1559–1959. Exposição bibliográfica. Évora 1959. pp.[vi].453. [1381.]

Exeter college, Oxford.

[LEWIS RICHARD FARNELL], Bibliography of the fellows and tutors of Exeter college, Oxford, in

recent times. Oxford [printed] [1914]. pp.[iv].67.
[1000.]
  *privately printed; the British museum copy contains
ms. corrections.*

Fisk university.

FISK university theses, 1917–1942, available for
inter-library loan. Nashville, Tenn. 1942. ff.[i].29.
[225.]*

Florida, university of.

CURRENT research and publications. Gainesville.
1943–1944. pp.53. [350.]

GRADUATE theses and dissertations. University
of Florida library: Gainesville.*
    1906–1938. ff.[ii].35. [450.]
    1939–1945. ff.[iii].30. [340.]
    1946–1951. By Clyde Miller. University of
        Florida: Libraries: Bibliographic series
        (no.1). pp.100. [800.]*

Fort Hays Kansas state college.

PAUL K. FRIESNER, Bibliography of master's
theses . . . 1930–1962. Fort Hays studies: Bibliography series (no.2): [Hays] 1962. pp.ix.116.

Franeker, university of.

EMO LUCIUS VRIEMOET, Athenarvm frisiacarvm libri duo. Leobardiae 1758. pp.[xvi].cxii.[vii].920. 24. [2500.]

the second book is devoted to the professors of the university of Franeker.

Frankfort on the Oder, university of.

GUSTAV BAUCH, Das älteste decanatsbuch der philosophischen fakultät an der universität zu

Frankfurt a. O. Erster theil. Die artistisch-philosophischen promotionen von 1506 bis 1540. Breslau 1897. pp.84. [69.]

Fribourg, university of.

N[ICOLAS] WEYRICH, Les thèses de doctorat à l'université de Fribourg depuis sa fondation en 1889 jusqu'au 1er mars 1936. Fribourg 1936. pp. xi.128.

Geneva, university of.

CH[ARLES] LE FORT, Catalogues des thèses soutenues devant la faculté de droit de Genève de 1821 à 1877. Genève 1878. pp.32. [208.]

A[UGUSTE] BOUVIER, La faculté de théologie de Genève pendant le dix-neuvième siècle. Thèses-concours-étudiants. Documents pour servir à l'histoire de l'académie de Genève (vol.i): Genève 1878. pp.viii.96. [280.]

[EUGÈNE RITTER], Catalogue des ouvrages, articles et mémoires publiés par les professeurs de l'université de Genève. Documents pour servir à l'histoire de l'université de Genève (vol.iii): Genève 1883. pp.viii.112. [1500.]

[—] — [second edition]. Catalogue . . . de Genève, ainsi que des thèses présentées de 1873 à 1895 aux diverses facultés pour l'obtention des grades universitaires. Rassemblé . . . par Charles Soret. . . . (vol.iv): 1896. pp.viii.402. [6000.]

[—] — — [supplements].

1896–1907. Par Charles Julliard. . . . (vol.v): 1909. pp.xiii.407. [6000.]

1908–1913. Par Albert Kohler. . . . (vol.vi): 1916. pp.xci.484. [6000.]

1914–1926. Par Albert Roussy. . . . (vol.vii): 1928. pp.viii.740. [10,000.]

1927–1937. Par Hermann Blanc. . . . (vol.viii): 1938. pp.viii.864. [12,000.]

1938–1942. . . . (vol.ix): 1944. pp.viii.579. [8000.]

1943–1947. . . . (vol.x): 1948. pp.viii.555.
[8000.]

1948–1952. . . . (vol.xi): 1953. pp.viii.719.
[10,000.]

1953–1957. . . . (vol.xii): 1959. pp.[vii].881.
[9000.]

in progress.

HENRI HEYER, Catalogue des thèses de théologie soutenues à l'académie de Genève pendant les XVIᵉ, XVIIᵉ et XVIIIᵉ siècles. Documents pour servir à l'histoire de l'académie de Genève (vol.v): Genève 1898. pp.cxi.168. [476.]

George Peabody college for teachers.

ABSTRACTS of dissertations. Nashville, Tenn. 1942 &c.

George Washington university.

BIBLIOGRAPHY. Titles of books . . . etc., published by members of the faculties, doctors of philosophy and doctors of civil law. George Washington university: Washington 1904. pp.[ii].59. [1500.]

Ghent, university of.

PAUL BERGMANS, Bibliographie des thèses de doctorat spécial soutenues devant l'université de

Gand. Gand 1895. pp.17. [23.]

THEO LUYKX, *ed.* Rijksuniversiteit te Gent. Liber memorialis 1913–1960. Universiteit: Rectoraat: Gent 1960 &c.
in progress.

Giessen, university of.

ADOLF KNIPPER and ERWIN SCHMIDT, Bibliographie zur geschichte der universität Giessen. Universitätsbibliothek: Berichte und arbeiten (no.2): Giessen 1963. pp.vii.77.

Glasgow, university of.

SUMMARIES of theses approved for higher degrees in the Faculty of science during the academical year. Glasgow.
    1949–1950. pp.vii.56. [35.]
    1950–1951. pp.vii.52. [33.]

1893–1905.   pp.ix.182+vii.122+vii.171+v.393 +[v].390+ix.176. [7500.]
privately printed.

[M. ELSAS], Glamorgan county record office exhibition. . . . Guide. [Cardiff 1958]. pp.20. [90.]

Gothenburg, university of.

GÖTEBORGS universitets bibliografi. Göteborg.
  1954–1956. 1959. pp.60. [800.]
in progress?

Göttingen, university of.

JOHANN FRIEDRICH BLUMENBACH, Synopsis
systematica scriptorvm qvibvs inde ab inavgvratione Academiae Georgiae Avgvstae d. xvii Sept.
MDCCXXXVII vsque ad sollemnia istivs inavgvrationis semisaecvlaria MDCCLXXXVII disciplinam
svam avgere et ornare stvdvervnt professores
medici gottingenses. Gottingae 1788. pp.36. [500.]

Groningen, university of.

H. M. MENSONIDES and A. T. SCHUITEMA MEIJER,
Inventaris der archieven van den senat, de facul-
teiten en het college van curatoren der Groning-
sche universiteit. Groningen 1947. pp.92. [large
number.]

Halle, university of.

CHRISTOPH WEIDLICH, Vollständiges verzeichniss aller auf der Königl. preussl. Friedrichs-
universität zu Halle . . . herausgekommenen

juristischen disputationen und programmen. Halle 1789. pp.xii.151.74. [1500.]

HALLESCHES akademisches vademecum. Erster band. Bio-bibliographie der aktiven professoren, privatdozenten u. lektoren der vereinigten Friedrichs-universität Halle-Wittenberg. Halle (Saale) 1910. pp.vi.306. [5000.]
no more published.

WOLFRAM SUCHIER, Bibliographie der universitätsschriften von Halle-Wittemberg 1817–1885, nebst einem anhang enthaltend die ausserordentlichen und ehrenpromotionen sowie die diplomerneuerungen. Universitäts- und landsbibliothek Sachsen-Anhalt: Arbeiten (vol.3): Berlin 1953. pp.xxiii.806. [5620.]

Harvard university.

LIST of the Publications of Harvard university and its officers [*afterwards:* with the chief publications on the university]. Harvard university: Library: Bibliographical contributions (no.12 &c.): Cambridge, Mass.

    1870–1880 . . . (no.12): 1881. pp.51. [2000.]
    1880–1885 . . . (no.21): 1886. pp.[ii].62. [2000.]

1885–1886. By William H. Thillinghast . . .
(no.23): 1887. pp.21. [600.]
1886–1887 . . . (no.28): 1888. pp.34. [1000.]
1887–1888 . . . (no.33): 1889. pp.28. [750.]
1888–1889 . . . (no.38): 1890. pp.29. [750.]
1889–1890 . . . (no.41): 1891. pp.32. [1000.]
1890–1891 . . . (no.44): 1892. pp.36. [1000.]
1891–1892 . . . (no.47): 1893. pp.34. [1000.]

HENRY C[LAY] BADGER, Mathematical theses of junior and senior classes, 1782–1839. Harvard university: Library: Bibliographical contributions (no.32): Cambridge, Mass. 1888. pp.14. [406.]

ANDREW MCFARLAND DAVIS, An analysis of the early records of Harvard college, 1636–1750. Harvard university: Library: Bibliographical contributions (no.50): Cambridge, Mass. 1895. pp.19. [200.]

DOCTORS of philosophy and doctors of science who have received their degree in course from Harvard university, 1873–1926, with the titles of their theses. Harvard university: Official register (vol.xxiii, no.39): Cambridge, Mass. 1926. pp.199. [1506.]

C. E. WALTON, Harvard university archives. Tercentenary exhibition. An historical prospect of Harvard college, 1636–1936. Society for the preservation of New England antiquities: Boston 1936. pp.48. [300.]

[ZOLTÁN HARASZTI], The Harvard tercentenary. An exhibit of rare books, manuscripts, . . . relating to the history of Harvard college. Public library: Boston 1936. pp.22. [300.]

DOCTORS of philosophy. Harvard university and Radcliffe college, with the titles of their theses [Cambridge, Mass.]
    1945–1946. pp.   . [92.]
    1947–1948. pp.   . [226.]
no more published.

CURRENT projects and publications. Harvard university: Russian research center: Cambridge 1955. pp.[v].46. [300.]

Havana, university of.

CARLOS MANUEL TRELLES Y GOVÍN, Bibliografía de la universidad de la Habana. Habana 1938. pp.337. [4500.]

Hawaii, university of.

BIBLIOGRAPHICAL list of the publications by members of the faculty [List of publications: Publications distributed by the university of Hawaii publication division; Bibliography issue, university publications; Bibliography]. Honolulu.

1925–1927. pp.11. [100.]
1928.
1929. pp.[4]. [20.]
1930.
1931.
1932.
1933.
1934.
1935. ff.2. [50.]★
1936. ff.[2]. [70.]★
1937.
1938.
1939–1943. pp.54. [1000.]
1943–1944. pp.15. [125.]
1944–1952. Edited by Charles S. Bouslog. pp.174. [2500.]
1952–1954. pp.64. [750.]
1954–1956. pp.64. [750.]
1956–1959. pp.52. [900.]
in progress.

Hebrew university.
רשימת הפירסומים המדעיים של העובדים

Special Subjects

האקדימיים; במדעי-הרוח, משפטים, מתי-
מטיקה ומדעי-הטבע, וחקלאות, תשי"נ-
תשי"ו. ירושלים, תשי"ב. A list of publications in
humanities, law, science and agriculture 1946–
1952, by members of the academic staff. [Jeru-
salem 1953]. pp.192. [1500.]

HENRY V. BESSO, Bibliografía sobre el judeo-
español. Mexico [1952]. pp.7. [134.]

Helsinki university.

VERZEICHNIS der im studienjahre ... erschienenen akademischen schriften der Kaiserl. Alexan-
ders-universität in Finnland (Helsingfors). [1916/
1917–1918/1919: der universität Finnlands; 1919/
1920–1938: der universität Helsingfors]. [Hel-
sinki].

    1903–1904. pp.[2]. [25.]
    1904–1905. pp.[2]. [25.]
    1905–1906. pp.[3]. [30.]
    1906–1907. pp.[3]. [30.]
    1907–1908. pp.[3]. [25.]
    1908–1909. pp.[2]. [25.]
    1909–1910. pp.[2]. [20.]
    1910–1911. pp.[2]. [25.]
    1911–1912. pp.[3]. [35.]
    1912–1913. pp.

Special Subjects

1913–1914. pp.
1914–1915. pp.[3]. [30.]
1915–1916. pp.[2]. [25.]
1916–1917. pp.[2]. [25.]
1917–1918. pp.[2]. [15.]
1918–1919. pp.[3]. [30.]
1919–1920. pp.[4]. [40.]
1920–1921. pp.[3]. [30.]
1921–1922. pp.[2]. [20.]
1922–1923. pp.[3]. [35.]
1923–1924. pp.[3]. [30.]
1924–1925. pp.[3]. [30.]

1925–1926. pp.[3]. [25.]
1926–1927. pp.[4]. [40.]
1927–1928. pp.[3]. [30.]
1928–1929. pp.[3]. [30.]
1929–1930. pp.[4]. [40.]
1930–1931. pp.[4]. [40.]
1931–1932. pp.[4]. [40.]
1932–1933. pp.[4]. [40.]
1933–1934. pp.[3]. [35.]
1934–1935. pp.[4]. [40.]
1935–1936. pp.[4]. [35.]
1936–1937. pp.[4]. [55.]
1937–1938. pp.[4]. [45.]

TOR [HAROLD] CARPELAN and L[AURI] O[SKAR]

TH[EODOR] TUDEER, Helsingfors universitet. Lärare och tjänstemän från år 1828. Helsingfors 1925 [1921–1926]. pp.viii.502+[iv].503–1128. [12,500.]

[LIV] IRIS ROOS[-HASSELBLATT], Helsingin yliopiston väitöskirjat ja ohjelmat vuosina 1909–1928. Helsingin yliopiston kirjaston julkaisuja (vol.xiii): Helsinki 1930. pp.xiv.99. [500.]

LIST of academical publications issued at the university of Helsinki.
    1957–1958. pp.5. [60.]
    1958–1959. pp.6. [75.]

Houston, university of.

RUTH S. WIKOFF, DORIS BATEMAN and JOAN BELK, Bibliography of theses and dissertations . . . for advanced degrees at the university of Houston, 1940–1958. Houston 1959. pp.v.42. [538.]

Howard university.

DOROTHY B[URNETT] PORTER, Howard university masters' theses submitted in partial fulfillment of the requirements for the masters' degree at Howard university, 1918–1945. pp.44. [544.]

Hull, university of.

ABSTRACTS of theses for higher degrees, September 1954 to July 1960. Hull 1961. pp.vii.55. [45.]

Idaho, university of.

CHARLES A. WEBBERT, Bibliography of masters' theses. . . . 1898–1958. University of Idaho: Bookmark (vol.11, no.2, supplement): Moscow 1958. pp.iv.92. [1917.]

Illinois, university of.

BOOKS and articles published by the corps of instruction [Books, articles and reviews published by the faculty; List of publications of the faculty]. Urbana 1912–1913 — 1947–1948.

no more published; early lists form part of the University studies: Miscellaneous series.

RUSSELL T[AAFFE] GREGG and THOMAS T[RISTAM] HAMILTON, Annotated bibliography of graduate

theses in education at the university of Illinois. [University of Illinois:] College of education: Bureau of educational research: Bulletin (no.55): Urbana 1931. pp.80.

PUBLICATIONS 1904–1956, university of Illinois, Engineering experiment station. A cumulative index. University of Illinois: Bulletin (vol.liii, no.54): Urbana 1956. pp.40. [554.]

Indiana university.

STUDIES in education [*afterwards:* Thesis abstract series]. Indiana university: School of education: Studies in education: Bloomington 1945–1949 &c.
in progress; details of this work are entered under Academic writings: Education, above.

Ingolstadt, university of.

FRANZ SALES ROMSTÖCK, Die jesuitennullen Prantl's an der universität Ingolstadt und ihre leidensgenossen. Eine biobibliographische studie. Eichstätt 1898. pp.viii.523. [2500.]

Iowa state university.

ROSTER, doctors of philosophy, 1916–1935. Iowa state college of agriculture and mechanic arts: Ames 1934. pp.44. [250.]

WILLIAM L[UTHER] HUNTER, Theses pertaining to industrial arts education, Iowa state college, 1922–1935. [Ames 1935]. ff.[iv].18. [106.]*

A LIST of research reports, master and doctoral theses, 1955 to 1959, College of engineering. Iowa

Special Subjects

state university of science and technology: Ames [1960]. pp.[iii].11. [331.]*

Iowa, university of.

[BERTHA G. RIDGWAY], A bibliography of the publications of the university and its members. Bulletin of the State university of Iowa (n.s., no.7): Iowa City 1900. pp.64. [600.]

— — 1900–1912. [By Malcolm G. Wyer]. . . . (no.67): 1913. pp.74. [2000.]

— — University bibliography, 1913–1916. [By Jane E. Roberts]. University of Iowa monographs (no.9): 1917. pp.41. [1000.]

— — 1917 . . . (no.20): 1918. pp.20. [400.]

— — 1918–1920. University of Iowa studies (no.49): 1921. pp.32. [750.]

GRADUATE theses. University of Iowa: Studies (1st ser., no.101): Iowa City 1926. pp.[31]. [750.]

DOCTORAL dissertations. Abstracts and references. University of Iowa studies (n.s. no.392 = Aims and progress of research, no.66): Iowa City.

i. 1900–1937 . . . (no.392 = . . . 66): 1940. pp.267. [850.]

Istanbul, university of.

ADNAN ÖTÜKEN, Istanbul üniversitese yayınları

biblyografyasī, 1933–1945. Ankara 1947. pp.446. [616.]

EDEBİYAT fakültesi yayınları kataloğu. İstanbul 1952. pp.[iii].155. [1000.]

Jagiellonian university.

ANNA ŻELEŃSKA–CHEŁKOWSKA, Inwentarz akt senatu i władz nadrzędnych oraz wydziałow Uniwersytetu jagiellońskiego, 1796–1849. Universytet jagielloński: Archiwum: Inwentarze i katalogi (ser. B, vol.i): Kraków 1962. pp.xii.143. [large number.]

— — Józef Zieliński, Inwentarz akt senatu akademickiego Uniwersytetu jagiellońskiego, 1849–1939. . . . (vol.ii): 1963. pp.130. [large number.]

Jena, university of.

JOHANN CASPAR ZEUMER, Vitæ professorvm theolog. omnivm, qvi in illvstri Academia ienensi ab ipsivs fvndatione ad nostra vsque tempora vixervnt, vna cum scriptis ab ipsis editis recensitæ. Ienæ [1703]. pp.[vi].266. [2500.]

JOHANN CASPAR ZEUMER, Vitæ professorvm ivrivm, qvi in illvstri Acadmia [*sic*] ienensi ab ipsivs fvndatione ad nostra vsque tempora vixervnt, vna cvm scriptis ab ipsis editis recensitæ.

Ienæ [1706]. pp.[ii].197. [1000.]

BARTHOLOMAEUS CHRISTIAN RICHARD [REI-CHARD], Commentatio de vita et scriptis pro-fessorvm hodie in Academia ienensi pvblice docentivm. Iena 1710. pp.[vi].120. [1500.]

JOHANN CASPAR ZEUMER, Vitæ professorvm theologiae, ivrisprvdentiae, medicinae et philoso-phiae qvi in illvstri Academia ienensi ab ipsivs fvndatione ad nostra vsqve tempora vixervnt et adhvc vivvnt, una cvm scriptis a qvolibet editis. Ienae 1711. pp.[xvi].302.272.112.248. [5000.]

VERZEICHNISS der während eines zeitraums von 25 jahren aus dem Chemischen universitäts-laboratorium zu Jena unter der direction des professor dʳ A. Geuther hervorgegangenen arbei-ten. Jena 1888. pp.14. [151.]

Jews' college.

[RUTH LEHMANN], Jews' college, London, cen-tenary celebration. . . . Catalogue of an exhibition of books by members of the academic staff and alumni. 1955. pp.16. [200.]

RUTH P. LEHMANN, History of Jews' college library 1860–1960. [1960]. pp.[iv].28. [400.]

consists in large part of a list of writings by members of the college.

Johns Hopkins university.

BIBLIOGRAPHIA hopkinsiensis, 1876–1891 [1893]. Baltimore 1892–1894. pp.[iii].52+vi.50+vii.57. [3500.]

EDWARD B[ENNETT] MATHEWS and G. E. REED, Bibliography of the faculty and students of the Department of geology of the Johns Hopkins university, 1883–1913. Baltimore 1913. pp.143. [2750.]

LIST of dissertations submitted in partial fulfillment of the requirements for the degree of doctor of philosophy in the Johns Hopkins university, 1878–1919. Johns Hopkins university circular (new ser. 1920, no.1 = whole no.321): Baltimore 1920. pp.96. [1093.]

— [another edition]. List of dissertations submitted in conformity with the requirements for the degrees of doctor of philosophy, doctor of engineering, and doctor of science in hygiene. . . . 1876–1926. . . . (new ser. 1926, no.8 = whole no.373): 1926. pp.85. [1437.]

Kansas, university of.

TITLES to theses presented in partial fulfillment of the requirements for advanced degrees in the graduate school. University of Kansas: [Lawrence] 1920. pp.43. [600.]

MARY MAUD SMELSER, List of publications. University of Kansas: Bulletin (vol.36, no.12 = Library series, no.1): Lawrence 1935. pp.127. [1500.]

UNIVERSITY of Kansas graduate school theses. University of Kansas. . . . Publications: Library series (no.2 &c.).
> 1888–1947. By Bessie E. Wilder. . . . (no.2):
> 1949. pp.305. [3000.]
> 1948–1958. . . . (no.12): 1961. pp.233. [2500.]

Kansas state teachers college.

AN ANNOTATED bibliography of theses accepted for the master of science degree. State teachers college: Studies in education (no.17 &c.): Emporia.
> 1929–1939. Edited by E[dwin] J[ohn] Brown, Henry E. Schrammel and Irene Niler. . . . (no.17): 1939. pp.61. [250.]
> 1939–1944. Edited by John Brenkelman . . . (no.29): 1944. pp.32. [725.]

Kansas state university.

LIST of faculty publications 1961 and 1962. Kansas state university: Manhattan 1963. pp.[iii]. 96. [1200.]*

Karachi, university of.

[MUSSAWIR ALI HAMIDI], Bibliography of theses, dissertations & research reports, university of Karachi. West Pakistan bureau of education: Bibliographical series (no.iii): Lahore [1962]. ff. [ii].16. [161.]*

Kazakhsky gosudarstvennuiy universitet.

R. F. VASILENKO and V. N. PAZDMIKOV, Библиографический сборник Казахского государственного универсітета им. С. М. Кирова. Алма-Ата 1957. pp.178. [2273.]
— — [second edition].
Библиографический указатель трудов сотрудников Казахского государственного университета им. С. М. Кирова. [&c.]. [By E. E. Trunova, U. Kudekova and N. P. Nesterova]. 1961. pp.375. [3781.]

Kazan, university of.

E. M. MISHINA, Систематический указатель статей к периодическим изданиям Казанского ... государственного университета им. В. И. Ульянова-Ленина, 1815–1947 гг. Казань 1960. pp.280. [4659.]

Kent state university.

ABSTRACTS of theses, Kent state university, 1952–1953. Kent, O. 1953. pp.[xiv].134. [125.]*

Kentucky, university of.

RESEARCH publications of members of the Research club. [Lexington] 1929. pp.59. [1000.]

THESES and dissertations presented in partial fulfillment of the requirements for advanced degrees at the university of Kentucky during the years 1925 to 1937 inclusive. [Lexington] 1938. pp.59.

LIST of publications of the members of the university of Kentucky staff. University of Kentucky: Margaret I. King library: Occasional contributions (no.8 &c.): [Lexington].*

1938–1948. . . . (no.8): 1950. ff.79. [1500.]
1948–1949. . . . (no.18): [1950]. ff.12. [250.]
1949–1950. . . . (no.27): 1951. pp.18. [350.]
1950–1951. . . . (no.35): 1952. pp.15. [300.]
1951–1952. . . . (no.55): 1953. pp.[ii].18. [350.]
1952–1953. . . . (no.64): 1954. pp.[i].13. [300.]
1953–1954. . . . (no.70): 1955. pp.[ii].13. [300.]
1954–1955. . . . (no.79): 1956. pp.[ii].17. [250.]
1955–1956. . . . (no.87): 1957. pp.[ii].14. [200.]
[*continued as:*]

University of Kentucky research publications.
Kentucky research foundation and University of
Kentucky: Library: [Lexington].

1956–1957. pp.19. [500.]
1957–1958. pp.27. [750.]
1958–1959. pp.27. [750.]
1959. pp.23. [750.]
1960. pp.28. [850.]
1961. pp.27. [800.]
in progress.

Kiel, university of.

JOHANN OTTO THIESS, Gelehrtengeschichte der
universität zu Kiel. [Biographische und biblio-
graphische nachrichten von allen bisherigen (von
den neuern) lehrern der theologie]. Kiel 1800–
1803. pp.xl.472+[iii].xii.450. [5000.]

Lamar state college of technology.

BIBLIOGRAPHY of faculty writing, January, 1956 to December, 1961. [Beaumont, Texas] 1962. pp.[i].16. [250.]*

Leeds university.

PUBLICATIONS and abstracts of theses by members of the university. Leeds.

    1927–1928. pp.31. [300.]
    1928–1929. pp.40. [400.]
    1929–1930. pp.54. [400.]
    1930–1931. pp.28. [300.]
    1931–1932. pp.26. [350.]
    1932–1933. pp.31. [300.]
    1933–1934. pp.34. [450.]

    1934–1935. pp.34. [400.]
    1935–1936. pp.29. [300.]
    1936–1937. pp.27. [300.]
    1937–1938. pp.31. [350.]
no more published.

PUBLICATIONS and titles of theses. University of Leeds: [Leeds].

    1950–1951. 1954. pp.53. [500.]
    1951–1952. 1954. pp.57. [500.]

1952–1953. 1955. pp.76. [600.]
1953–1954. 1957. pp.70. [600.]
1954–1955. 1957. pp.73. [600.]
1955–1956. 1958. pp.74. [600.]
1956–1957. 1959. pp.77. [600.]
1957–1958. 1960. pp.74. [600.]
1958–1959. 1961. pp.79. [700.]
1959–1960. 1962. pp.75. [600.]
1960–1961. 1963. pp.84. [700.]

in progress.

Lehigh university.

BIBLIOGRAPHY and abstracts [abstract; abstracts] of the publications of Lehigh university faculty members. Lehigh university publications (vol.12, no.1 &c.): Bethlehem, Pa.

i. 1935.... (vol.12, no.1): 1938. pp.64. [320.]
ii. 1938.... vol.13, no.1): 1939. pp.39. [150.]
iii. 1939. 1940. pp.48. [175.]
iv. 1940... (vol.xv, no.2): 1941. pp.37. [125.]
v. 1941–1942.... (vol.xix, no.2): 1945. pp.52. [200.]
vi. 1943–1946. . . . (vol.xxi, no.2): 1947. pp.54. [250.]
vii. 1947. . . . (vol.xxii, no.2): 1948. pp.24. [125.]

viii. 1948. . . . (vol.xxiii, no.2): 1949. pp.29.
[150.]
no more published.

Leipzig, university of.

H[EINRICH] G[OTTLIEB] KREUSSLER, *ed.* Auto-
biographieen leipziger gelehrten. Leipzig [1810].
pp.[iii].78. [1000.]

VERZEICHNIS der an der universität Leipzig
erschienenen dissertationen und fakultätsschriften
auf englischem gebiet. [Leipzig 1900]. pp.7. [150.]
covers works published during the period 1875–1900.

[EDITH ROTHE and HILDEGARD HEILEMANN],
Karl-Marx-universität Leipzig. Bibliographie zur
universitätsgeschichte 1409–1959. Sächsische aka-
demie der wissenschaften: Historische kommission: Schriften (vol.36 = Bibliographie der stadt
Leipzig, vol.ii): Leipzig 1961. pp.558. [8000.]

Leningrad, university of.

КАТАЛОГ изданий имеющихся в наличии
(1946–1955 гг.). [Leningrad] 1955. pp.72. [200.]

A. G. MALAKHOV, Каталог изданий, 1950–
1956. [Leningrad] 1956. pp.51. [150.]

[N. N. KURUKOVA], Диссертации, защищенные в Ленинградском ордена Ленина государственном университете имени А. А. Жданова в 1955 году. Библиографический указатель. Ленинградский ордена Ленина государственный университет имени А. А. Жданова: Научная библиотека имени М. Горького: Ленинград 1956. pp.58. [350.]

[L. G. BERNSTAMM, N. N. KURUKOVA and L. A. SHILOV], Систематический указатель к периодическим изданиям С.-Петербургского — Ленинградского университета, 1876–1956. Ленинградский... государственный университет имени А. А. Жданова: Научная библиотека имени М. Горького: Москва 1959. pp.446. [5834.]

A. KH. GORFUNKEL, L. A. NIKULINA and S. N. SEMANOV, Материалы по истории Ленинградского университета, 1819–1917, Обзор архивных документов: [Leningrad] 1961. pp.124. [1500.]

Lietuvos TSR mokslų akademija.

LIETUVOS TSR mokslų akademijos ir jos mokslo darbuotojų leidiniu bibliografija. Vilnius.

1941–1954. Sudarė: J. Basiulis, A. Bielinis ir
S. Kisielienė. pp.93. [359.]

1955. Sudarė: J. Basiulis ir A. Sitnikaitė. pp.
235. [1369.]

1958. Sudarė: A. Sitnikaitė ir A. Syvienė.
pp.239. [1259.]

1959. pp.251. [1446.]

1960. pp.224. [1326.]

in progress.

V[LADAS] ABRAMAVIČIUS and K. ĆEPIENĖ, Lietuvos TSR mokslų akademijos rankraštinių darbų ir

disertarijų bibliografija, 1946–1956. Vilnius 1959.
pp.159. [633.]

J. BASIULIS and A. SITNIKAITĖ, Lietuvos TSR
mokslų akademijos darbuotojų straipsnių bibliografija 1945–1954. Vilnius 1960. pp.408. [2712.]

Litoral, Universidad nacional del.

FERNANDO L. GASPAR, Crónica bibliográfica de
las publicaciones de la Facultad de ciencias mate-
máticas de la Universidad nacional del Litoral.
Rosario 1940. pp.10. [9.]

Liverpool, university of.

TITLES of theses accepted for higher degrees. University of Liverpool.

    i. 1950. pp.3. [52.]

    [ii]. 1950–1951. pp.4. [70.]

    [iii]. 1951–1952. pp.4. [64.]

    [iv]. 1952–1953. pp.6. [99.]

Livingstone college.

LOUISE M. ROUNTREE, An annotated bibliography on Livingstone college including the presidents and college-church history. Salisbury, N.C. 1963. ff.[15]. [150.]*

Lodz, university of.

JANINA RACIEKA, Uniwersytet Łódzki w pierwszym dziesięcioleciu 1945–1954. Materiały bibliograficzne. Uniwersytet w Łódzi: Biblioteka: Wydawnictwa bibliograficzne (no.2): Wrocław 1955. pp.xxiv.233. [4115.]

London, university of.

LIST of doctoral theses and examination statistics. [c.1904]. pp.23.

covers the period *1886–1903.*

SUBJECTS of dissertations and theses and published work presented by successful candidates at examinations for higher degrees. University of London.

    1937–1944. pp.130. [2500.]
    1945. pp.[14]. [250.]
    1946. pp.15. [250.]
    1947. pp.23. [400.]
    1948. pp.29. [600.]
    1949. pp.31. [600.]
    1950. pp.35. [600.]
    1951. pp.30. [500.]
    1951–1952. pp.42. [750.]
    1952–1953. pp.48. [750.]
    1953–1954. pp.vi.46. [750.]
         [*continued as:*]

Theses and dissertations accepted for higher degrees.

    1954–1955. pp.vi.53. [900.]
    1955–1956. pp.vi.48. [800.]
    1956–1957. pp.vi.50. [900.]
    1957–1958. pp.iv.52. [1000.]
    1958–1959. pp.iv.52. [1000.]
    1959–1960. pp.iv.53. [1000.]
    1960–1961. pp.iv.54. [1000.]

1961–1962. pp.iv.55. [1200.]
1962–1963. pp.iv.62. [1250.]
in progress.

A[LBERT] H[UGH] SMITH and A[RTHUR] T[HOMAS] HATTO, A list of english, scandinavian and german theses in the university of London. London mediæval studies: Monograph (no.2): 1939. pp. viii.40. [403.]

Longwood college.

MARTHA HOLMAN JENKINS, Faculty publications. Longwood college: Farmville, Va. 1953. ff.23.

Louisiana state university.

ABSTRACTS of theses. . . . Louisiana state university: University bulletin (n.s. vol.xxviii, no.12, &c.): Baton Rouge.
  1935–1936. [By James Ellis Palmer]. . . .
    (n.s. vol.xxviii, no.12). pp.xiv.130. [175.]
  1936–1937. [By H. Leslie McKenzie]. . . .
    (vol.xxx, no.3). pp.xvii.130. [125.]
  1937–1938. [By A. B. Bonds]. . . . (vol.xxxi,
    no.1). pp.xvi.165. [225.]
  1938–1939. . . . (vol.xxxii, no.1). pp.xix.210.
    [300.]

1939–1940. . . . (vol.xxxiii, no.1). pp.xv.198. [250.]

1940–1941. . . . (vol.xxxiv, no.1). pp.xix.175. [190.]

1941–1942. . . . (vol.xxxv, no.1). pp.xii.102. [200.]

1942–1943. . . . (vol.xxxvi, no.1). pp.viii.59. [75.]

1943–1944. [By Eugenia Arnold Riefner and Helen Hutchinson]. . . . (vol.xxxvii, no.7). pp.45. [70.]

1944–1946. [By Gwen R. Haymon]. . . . (vol.xxxix, no.6). pp.71. [100.]

1946–1947. . . . (vol.xl, no.3). pp.76. [125.]

1947–1948. . . . (vol.xli, no.3). pp.90. [150.]

1948–1949. . . . (vol.xlii, no.3). pp.ix.52. [150.]

1949–1950. . . . (vol.xliii, no.3). pp.[xi].91. [250.]

1950–1952. . . . (vol.45, no.2): 1953. pp.[xiii]. 150. [400.]

1952–1954. . . . (vol.47, no.2): 1955. pp.[xiii]. 161. [4000.]

in progress?

THESES and dissertations, Department of education, Louisiana state university, 1917–1960. [Baton Rouge] 1961. ff.[ii].44. [550.]*

Louvain, university of.

BIBLIOGRAPHIE académique. Université catholique: Louvain 1880. pp.[iv].311. [2500.]
— [third edition]. Bibliographie, 1834–1900. 1900. pp.xi.386. [4500.]
— — Supplements.
   i. 1899–1901. pp.iii–viii.74. [1000.]
   ii. 1901–1903. pp.iii–viii.92. [1000.]
   iii. 1903–1905. pp.vi.88. [1000.]
   [iv]. 1834–1908. pp.viii.333. [7500.]
   v. 1908–1911. pp.vi.100. [1500.]
   vi. 1911–1913. pp.vi.82. [1000.]
   vi[vii]. 1914–1934. 1937. pp.xvi.87.453. [8000.]

   vii[viii]. 1934–1954. Rédigée par J[oseph] Coppens et C[onstant Emiel] Vervoort. pp.444. [6000.]
   viii[ix]. 1954–1955. pp.228. [3000.]
   ix[x]. 1956. pp.216. [3000.]
in progress?

HUBERT NÉLIS, Inventaire des archives de l'Université de l'état à Louvain et du Collège philosophique (1817–1835). Inventaires des archives de la Belgique: Bruxelles 1917. pp.75. [2000.]

HENRI DE VOCHT, Inventaire des archives de l'université de Louvain, 1426–1797, aux Archives générales du royaume à Bruxelles. Inventaires des archives de la Belgique: Louvain 1927. pp.xlvii. 586. [100,000.]

Lucknow, university of.

ABSTRACTS of publications by members of the university. University of Lucknow: Lucknow.

    1921–1927. 1928. pp.[v].156. [500.]
    1928–1932. 1933. pp.[vii].244. [1000.]
    1933–1937. 1938. pp.[vii].352. [1500.]

Lund, university of.

[JOHAN] PONTUS SJÖBECK, Program utgifna vid Lunds universitet, 1667–1867. [Lund universitet: Årsskrift (new ser., part 1, vol.xi):] Lund &c. 1912–1915. pp.xxxii.143. [746.]

LUNDS universitets bibliografi. Lund.

    1941–1942. [By Erik J. Knudtzon]. pp.26. [550.]
    1942–1943. pp.23. [500.]
    1943–1944. pp.24. [500.]
    1944–1945. [By E. J. Knudtzon and Nils

T. A. G. Palmborg]. pp.24. [500.]
1945–1946. [By N. Palmborg]. pp.19. [350.]
1946–1947. pp.25. [500.]
1947–1948. pp.25. [500.]
1948–1949. pp.31. [500.]
1949–1950. pp.30. [500.]
1950–1951. pp.35. [500.]
1951–1952. pp.40. [600.]
1952–1953. pp.48. [800.]
1953–1954. 1956. pp.44. [1000.]
1954–1955. pp.50. [1000.]
1955–1956. pp.53. [1200.]
1956–1957. pp.55. [1200.]
1957–1958. pp.63. [1500.]
1958–1959. pp.62. [1200.]
1959–1960. pp.67. [1500.]

in progress.

ERIK LARSSON, Kemiska institutionen i Lund. Lärare och bibliografi, 1897–1956. Lund 1958. pp.41. [700.]

ENVOI de la bibliothèque de l'université royale de Lund.

1957–1958. pp.[3]. [40.]
1958–1959. pp.[3]. [40.]
1959–1960. pp.[3]. [40.]
1960–1961. pp.[4]. [55.]

1961–1962.
1962–1963. pp.[3]. [50.]
consists of a list of theses and publications; in progress.

Lvov, university of.

N[ATALIYA] R[OMANIVNA] BEREZHNA [*and others*], Друковані праці професорів, викладачів і співробітників Львіського університету за 1944–1960 роки. Бібліографічний покажчик. Львів 1962. pp.768. [7000.]

Madrid, university of.

CATÁLOGO de las tesis doctorales manuscritas existentes en la universidad de Madrid. Madrid 1952. pp.36. [1600.]

SUMARIOS y extractos de las tesis doctorales leidas . . . universidad de Madrid . . . 1939–1944 [–1950]. Facultad de filosofía y letras: Madrid 1953–1954. pp.305+3–416. [97.]

Magdalen college.

E. M. MAC FARLANE, Catalogus operum ab illustribus alumnis Collegii B. Mariæ Magdalenæ in academia Oxoniensi, scriptorum vel editorum

quibus aucta est bibliotheca . . . Joannis Rouse
Bloxam. Oxonii 1862. pp.[iii].155. [2250.]

*the running title is 'Appendix to the catalogue of
Magdalen college library'; a copy with ms. additions
by the author is in the Bodleian library.*

Marii Curie-Skłodowskiej, uniwersytet.

STEFANIA FEDORKO, Annales universitatis Curie-
Skłodowska. Bibliografia. Lublin 1959. pp.xxxi.
128. [906.]

Marshall college.

THESES and problem reports submitted in partial
fulfillment of the requirements for the master's
degree in Marshall college, from June, 1940
through June, 1953. Huntington, W.Va. 1953.
ff.[ii].23. [500.]*

Maryland, university of.

ABSTRACTS of theses for the degree of doctor of
philosophy, with the titles of theses accepted for
the master's degree, for the academic years 1938–
1939 and 1939–1940. University of Maryland:
Official publication (vol.xxxvii, no.9): College
Park 1940. pp.55. [34.]

RESEARCH in the university of Maryland 1953–1955. University of Maryland: Publication (vol.9, no.3): [College Park] 1956. pp.104. [1000.]

Massachusetts institute of technology.

KATHARINE MAYNARD and MURRAY F[RANK] GARDNER, A classified list of theses in electrical engineering presented at Massachusetts institute of technology, 1902–1929, including also recent research reports. Massachusetts institute of technology: Publication [vol.lxv, no.46 = Department of electrical engineering, no.65):] Cambridge 1929. pp.108. [1280.]

RALPH R[EGINALD] MCNAY, A subject list of theses in civil and sanitary engineering . . . 1913–1938. Massachusetts institute of technology: Library: Cambridge 1939. ff.68. [1600.]*

BARBARA KLINGENHAGEN, A subject list of theses presented by candidates for the degrees . . . in the courses . . . at Massachusetts institute of technology, 1917–1940. [Cambridge, Mass.] 1940. ff.[ii]. 167. [1800.]*

LIST of periodical publications, books and reviews by members of the staff and theses presented for doctors' degrees. Massachusetts institute of technology: Cambridge.

[1941–]1942. pp.32. [400.]

[1942–]1943. pp.23. [300.]

1943–1944. pp.24. [300.]

1944–1945. pp.23. [300.]

1945–1946. pp.25. [300.]

1946–1947. pp.34. [400.]

1947–1948. Edited by Margaret P. Hazen. pp.[ii].42. [500.]

1948–1949. pp.[ii].50. [600.]

1949–1950. pp.[ii].54. [700.]

1950–1951. pp.[ii].61. [800.]

[*continued as:*]

List . . . of the staff and the Division of industrial cooperation.

1951–1952. pp.63. [800.]

[*continued as:*]

Periodical publications [&c.].

1951–1952 [*sic,* 1952–1953]. pp.64. [800.]

[*continued as:*]

Publications from the institute.

1953–1954. pp.[iii].79. [1000.]

1954–1955. pp.[iii].107. [1200.]

1955–1956. pp.[ii].345–418. [1000.]

1956–1957. pp.[iii].66. [1200.]

[*continued as:*]

Publications and theses.

1957–1958. pp.[ii].109. [2000.]
1958–1959. pp.[iii].129. [2250.]
1959–1960.
1960–1961.
1961–1962. pp.[iii].143. [2500.]
in progress.

México, colegio de.

A DESCRIPTIVE list of research papers and theses accepted by the graduate school of Mexico city college. Centro de estudios universitarios: [Mexico].

[i]. 1947–1954. pp.3–48. [250.]
ii. 1954–1960. pp.3–37. [175.]
in progress.

Mexico, universidad de.

TOBÍAS CHÁVEZ, Notas para la bibliografía de las obras editadas o patrocinadas por la Universidad nacional autónoma de México. Contiene además las notas bibliográficas de las tesis presentadas por los graduados, durante los años de 1937 a 1942. México 1943. pp.260. [5000.]

FRANCISCO DE LA MAZA, Las tesis impresas de la antigua universidad de México. Universidad na-

cional autónoma de México: Instituto de investigaciones estéticas: México 1944. pp.26. [29.]

[OSCAR URIBE VILLEGAS and JOSÉ MARIA AVILÉS],
Catálogo de publicaciones. Universidad nacional:
Instituto de investigaciones sociales: México 1961.
pp.53. [77.]

Michigan state college.

PUBLICATIONS of Michigan state college staff
members. East Lansing.

    1942–1943. Compiled by Joseph George
       Duncan. pp.56. [750.]
    1943–1944.
    1944–1946.
    1946–1948.

Michigan, university of.

ALFRED H. LLOYD, Bibliography of publications
by members of the several faculties from . . .
1909, to . . . 1918. University of Michigan: University bulletin (new ser., vol.xxi, no.32): Ann
Arbor 1920. pp.[iii].104. [1750.]

ESTHER ANNE SMITH, University of Michigan
publications containing material of a scientific
or learned character. University of Michigan:

General library publication (no.2): Ann Arbor 1922. pp.[v].99. [287.]

ABSTRACTS of dissertations and theses in education at the university of Michigan. Bureau of educational reference and research: Ann Arbor.
> i. 1917–1931. [By Warren R. Good]. pp.vi. 137. [70.]
> ii. 1931–1932. pp.[vi].130. [110.]

Minnesota, university of.

SCIENTIFIC publications, including the publications of the Geological and natural history survey. University of Minnesota: Library: Minneapolis 1924. pp.11. [100.]

A REGISTER of the ph. d. degrees conferred by the university of Minnesota, 1888–1932. Minneapolis 1932. pp.vi.177. [644.]

— [second edition]. Register of ph. d. degrees conferred by the university of Minnesota, 1888 through June 1938. University of Minnesota: Bulletin (vol.xlii, no.31): 1939. pp.v.276. [1121.]

— — [supplement]. Register . . . 1938 through June 1956. 1957. pp.[ii].iv.365. [2700.]*

SUMMARIES of ph. d. theses. University of Minnesota: Minneapolis.
    i. [1924–1937]. 1939. pp.viii.343. [72.]
    ii. [1937–1939]. 1943. pp.[viii].285. [77.]
    iii. [1938–1940]. pp.[viii].253. [60.]
    iv. [1940–1941]. pp.[viii].257. [61.]
    v. [1940(*sic*)–1942]. pp.[viii].255. [60.]
no more published.

BIBLIOGRAPHY of publications resulting from research projects at the university of Minnesota, 1935–1941, conducted with the assistance of . . . Works projects administration. Minneapolis 1942. pp.[iii].66. [500.]*
— Supplement . . . 1942–February 1, 1943. 1943. ff.[i].19. [100.]*

PUBLICATIONS of the faculties. University of Minnesota: Bulletin (vol.xlviii, no.47 [&c.]: [Minneapolis].

    1944–1945 . . . (vol.xlviii, no.47): 1945. pp. iv.141. [3000.]
    1945–1946 . . . (vol.xlix, no.51): 1946. pp.[ii]. 130. [2500.]
    1946–1947 . . . (vol.l, no.53): 1947. pp.161. [3500.]

1947–1948 . . . (vol.li, no.52): 1948. pp.164. [3500.]

1948–1949 . . . (vol.lii, no.58): 1949. pp.221. [4500.]

1949–1950 . . . (vol.liii, no.61): 1950. pp.232. [4500.]

SUBJECTS of theses submitted by fellows in the Mayo foundation for medical education and research who obtained graduate degrees in the university of Minnesota from January, 1915, to July 1945. [Rochester 1945]. pp.55. [825.]

REGISTER of ph. d. degrees conferred by the university of Minnesota 1938 through June 1956. [Minneapolis] 1957. pp.[ii].iv.365. [2500.]*

Missouri, university of.

CHECK list of the official serial publications of the university. University of Missouri bulletin (vol.xv, no.2 = Library series, no.6): Columbia 1914. pp.44. [750.]

— Edition 4. Compiled by Ann Todd. . . . (vol.xlvi, no.15 = Library series, no.20): 1945. pp.255. [4000.]

GRADUATE school degrees conferred, 1892–1948. University of Missouri: Bulletin (vol.l, no.22 =

General series, 1949, no.19): Columbia 1949. pp. 154. [6550.]

w[ILLIAM] w[ESTON] CARPENTER and A[RLIE] G[LENN] CAPPS, Areas of educational administration considered in doctoral dissertations, university of Missouri. University of Missouri: Bulletin (vol.58, no.27): [Columbia] 1957. pp.51. [360.]

Montana, universities of.

BIBLIOGRAPHY of graduate theses, university of Montana, Montana state university, Montana state college, Montana school of mines. Montana historical records survey: Bozeman 1942. pp.vii. 71. [478.]*

FACULTY research publications. Montana state university: Missoula.
    [i]. 1942–1952. pp.32. [500.]
    ii. 1952–1957. pp.37. [600.]
in progress.

Montpellier, university of.

CARTULAIRE de l'université de Montpellier. Montpellier 1890–1912. pp.[vi].xxxix.759+[v]. clviii.930. [10,000.]

ANDRÉ GOURON, L'histoire de l'université des droits de Montpellier. Exposition. Faculté de droit: Montpellier 1963. pp.20. [100.]

Moscow, university of.

список изданий Московского гос. университета за 1875–1936 г.г. Москва 1936. pp.[ii]. 33+[ii].34–53. [400.]*

V. N. TERNOVSKY, Библиография диссертаций медицинского факультета Московского университета. Москва 1949. pp.64. [861.]
covers the period 1791–1922.

N. N. MELNIKOVA, Издания Московского университета, 1756–1779. Московский... государственный университет имени М. В. Ломоносова: [Москва] 1955. pp.251. [875.]

I. B. AGRANOVSKY [*and others*], Докторские и кандидатские диссертации защищенные в Московском государственном университете с 1934 по 1954 г. Библиографический указатель. Москва 1956–1960. pp.256+319+204. [3212.]

Nancy, university of.

MARIE MARCHAL, Catalogue des thèses soutenues devant la faculté de pharmacie de Nancy de 1873 à 1943. Université de Nancy: Nancy 1944. pp.48. [257.]

Nankai university.

PUBLICATIONS in english on economic and social China of the Nankai institute of economics, Nankai university. Tientsin 1937. pp.[ii].10. [40.]

Nebraska, university of.

JACOB HENRY GALLE, The learned and scientific publications of the university of Nebraska (1871–1926). Bibliographical contributions from the university of Nebraska library (vol.vi): Lincoln 1926. pp.130. [1500.]

LIST of publications by members of the faculty. Lincoln.

> 1925–1931. Compiled by Clara L[ouise] Craig and Ruby C[atherine] Wilder. Bibliographical contributions from the university of Nebraska library (vol.viii): 1932. pp.147. [2000.]

1931–1933 . . . (vol.ix): 1934. pp.92. [1250.]

1933–1935. University of Nebraska: Bulletin (series xli, no.8): 1936. pp.72. [1000.]

1935–1937 . . . (series xliii, no.5): 1938. pp.76. [1000.]

1937–1940. University of Nebraska publication . . . (no.141): 1942. pp.97. [1500.]

1941–1944. University of Nebraska publication (no.146): 1944. pp.52. [600.]

1944–1947 . . . (no.159): 1947. pp.[v].49. [1000.]

in progress.

SUMMARIES of doctoral dissertations and masters' theses accepted during 1936, Teachers college, university of Nebraska. University of Nebraska publication (no.121 = Educational monographs, no.10): Lincoln 1937. pp.40.

SUMMARIES of masters' theses in school administration, Teachers college, university of Nebraska, 1925–1940. University of Nebraska publications (no.136 = Educational monographs, no.15): Lincoln [1940]. pp.94.

ABSTRACTS of doctoral dissertations, the university of Nebraska. . . . To which is appended a list of the recipients of masters' degrees with the

thesis titles. Lincoln.
> 1940. pp.x.216. [190.]
> 1941. pp.xi.219. [200.]
> 1942. pp.xi.198. [150.]
> 1943. pp.ix.83. [90.]
> 1944. pp.ix.157. [60.]
> 1945. pp.ix.97. [70.]
> 1946. pp.ix.133. [120.]
> 1947. pp.[ix].66. [200.]
> 1948. pp.[xi].153. [250.]
> 1949. pp.[xi].212. [300.]
> 1950. pp.[xi].240. [300.]
> 1951. pp.[xi].303. [350.]
> 1952. pp.[xi].257. [300.]

in progress.

New York, university of the state of.

KAY KIRLIN MOORE, A checklist and index for the University of the state of New York bulletins, numbers 255–1094, June 1902 to June 1936. University of the state of New York: Bulletin (no.1152): Albany 1938. pp.371. [840.]

PUBLICATIONS of the faculty, State university of New York, College for teachers at Albany. [Albany] 1957. pp.[ii].50. [650.]*

M[ARY] E[LIZABETH] GRENANDER, A record of research and creative activity, State university of New York, July 1, 1948 to June 30, 1957. Albany 1958. pp.[ii].xi.160. [2613.]

New York city, college of.

ABSTRACTS of theses for the degree of master of science in education, 1923–1939. College of the city of New York: School of education: New York 1930. pp.118. [381.]

New York university.

UNIVERSITY bibliography. 1929–1930 &c.

HERBERT A[RTHUR] TONNE, Index of dissertations of the School of education. New York university. New York 1930. [630.]

—— [another edition]. 1932. pp.48. [1070.]

NOUVART TASHJIAN, *ed.* List of doctors' and masters' theses in education, New York university, 1890–June 1936. New York 1937. pp.[ii].ii-iii.117. [1565.]★

supplements have been issued.

New Zealand, university of.

D[AVID] L[LOYD] JENKINS, Union list of theses of

the university of New Zealand 1910–1954. New Zealand library association: Wellington 1956. pp. [279]. [3250.]*

North Carolina, university of.

CLYDE HULL CANTRELL, Graduate degrees awarded and titles of theses, 1894–1940. State college of agriculture and engineering: D. H. Hill library: Library studies (no.1 = State college record, vol.xl, no.12): Raleigh 1941. pp.58. [600.]

LIST of publications of the faculty, to June 30, 1943. Woman's college: Greensboro 1944. pp.24. [400.]

BOOKS from Chapel Hill. A complete catalogue 1923–1945. University of North Carolina sesquicentennial publications: Chapel Hill 1946. pp.xxvii.206. [600.]

JAMES L[OGAN] GODFREY, FLETCHER M[ELVIN] GREEN and W[ILLIAM] W[HATELY] PIERSON, The graduate school dissertations and theses. University sesquicentennial publications: Chapel Hill 1947. pp.184. [2668.]
— — First supplement: 1946–1959. University of North Carolina: Library studies (no.3): 1960. pp.[ix].371. [3486.]

CATHERINE M. MAYBURY, Publications of the
Institute of government, 1930–1956. [Chapel
Hill] 1957. ff.32. [250.]★
[—] — 1930–1962. By Olga C. Palotai. [1963].
pp.xvi.78. [750.]

FACULTY publications. University of North
Carolina: Woman's college: [Greensboro].
1959–1960. pp.13. [100.]★

North Dakota, university of.

BIBLIOGRAPHY of theses prepared at the university of North Dakota. North Dakota historical
records survey project: Bismarck 1940. pp.[vii].
68. [551.]★

Northern Illinois university.

FACULTY publications. Northern Illinois university: Research bulletin (no.3 &c.): [De Kalb].
1960. . . . (no.3). pp.[iii].65. [750.]★

Northwestern university.

A LIST of doctoral dissertations submitted at
the Northwestern university, 1896–1934. Chicago
1935. pp.27. [278.]

Notre Dame university.

[PHILIP SAMUEL MOORE, *ed.*], A selected list of publications of the faculty, 1843–1943. Bulletin (vol.xxxviii, no.1): Notre Dame 1943. pp.v.122. [2000.]

UNIVERSITY of Notre Dame publications and research. [Notre Dame, Ind.].*
1956–1957. ff.[ii].81. [1250.]*

Odessa, university of.

БІБЛІГРАФІЧНА серія. Одеса 1957 &c.
in progress.

Ohio state university.

A PARTIAL list of publications of former students of the Ohio state university. Columbus 1920. pp.143. [2000.]

ANNUAL list of publications. A selected list of the publications of the Ohio state university. Columbus.
　　i. 1928. pp.39. [500.]
　　i [*sic,* ii]. 1929. pp.39. [500.]

ABSTRACTS of doctoral dissertations. 1929 &c.

ABSTRACTS of masters' theses. Ann Arbor, Mich. 1935–1940.*

Oklahoma state university.

BOOKS, articles, reviews, patents and research interests of the faculty . . . October 1, 1945 to September 30, 1950. Stillwater [1950]. pp.82. [1500.]

Oregon state college.

RODNEY K. WALDRON and VIRGINIA FOLLOWELL, Theses and dissertations, 1943–1959. Oregon state college: Bibliographic series (no.6): Corvallis 1960. pp.139. [2075.]

Oregon, university of.

GEORGE N. BELKNAP, Publications of the university of Oregon, 1878–1937. Eugene 1938. pp.48. [400.]

GRADUATE theses, university of Oregon, Oregon state college, university of Oregon medical school, 1932–1942. Oregon state system of higher education: Eugene 1946. pp.ix.198.

Orléans, university of.

ORLÉANS. L'université et la typographie. Exposition. Société archéologique et historique de l'Orléanais: [Orléans] 1884. pp.xii.96. [university: 250.]

L'UNIVERSITÉ d'Orléans du XIIIe au XVIIIe siècle. [Orléans] 1961. pp.60. [165.]
an exhibition catalogue.

Oslo, university of.

KRONOLOGISK ordnet liste over memoranda fra Sosialøkonomisk institutt, universitetet i Oslo for perioden august 1947–juni 1958. [Oslo] 1958. ff.[32]. [400.]*

GUNNAR W. ANDRESEN, Doctores kreert ved universitetet i Oslo, 1817–1961. En bibliografi. Oslo 1962. pp.[iii].100. [489.]

Oxford, university of.

ABSTRACTS of dissertations for the degree of doctor of philosophy. University of Oxford: Committee for advanced studies: Oxford.

    i. [1927–1928]. pp.viii.144. [25.]
    ii. 1928–1929. pp.vii.170. [25.]
    iii. 1929–1930. pp.iv.110. [16.]
    iv. 1930–1931. pp.iv.100. [14.]
    v. 1931–1932. pp.iv.122. [17.]
    vi. 1932–1933. pp.v.304. [46.]
    vii. 1934. pp.iv:130. [25.]
    viii. 1935. pp.iv.182. [34.]

ix. 1936. pp.v.272. [48.]
x. 1937. pp.v.277. [43.]
xi. 1938. pp.v.306. [38.]
xii. 1939. pp.v.353. [47.]
xiii. 1940. 1947. pp.v.192. [39.]
no more published.

SUCCESSFUL candidates for the degrees of d. phil., b. litt., and b. sc. with titles of their theses. University of Oxford: Committee for advanced studies. Oxford.

i. 1940–1949. pp.56. [1000.]
ii. 1949–1950. pp.20. [300.]
iii. 1950–1951. pp.20. [300.]
iv. 1951–1952. pp.20. [300.]
v. 1952–1953. pp.24. [300.]
vi. 1953–1954. pp.22. [300.]
vii. 1954–1955. pp.23. [300.]
viii. 1955–1956. pp.23. [300.]
ix. 1956–1957. pp.23. [300.]
x. 1957–1958. pp.24. [300.]
xi. 1958–1959. pp.24. [300.]
xii. 1959–1960. pp.24. [300.]
xiii. 1960–1961. pp.24. [300.]
xiv. 1961–1962. pp.23. [300.]
xv. 1962–1963. pp.28. [350.]
in progress.

Pacific, college of the.

THESES accepted by the college in partial fulfillment of the requirements for the degree of
master of arts ... 1912–1939. College of the Pacific:
Stockton, Cal. 1940. ff.26. [178.]★

THESES and dissertations accepted in partial fulfillment of requirements for advanced degrees at
the College of the Pacific. Stockton, Cal.★
 1913–1956. [By Edith Grider]. pp.[v].69.
 [587.]
 1957–1960. [By James M. Perrin]. pp.[v].18.
 [194.]
in progress.

Padua, university of.

GIUSEPPE GIOMO, L'archivio antico della università di Padova. Venezia 1893. pp.88. [1000.]

ANTONIO FAVARO, Saggio di bibliografia dello
studio di Padova. Reale deputazione di storia
patria: Miscellanea di storia veneta (3rd sec.,
vols.xvi–xvii): Venezia 1922. pp.xi.457+[ii].416.
[6000.]

Panama, university of.

CARMEN D. DE HERRERA and OLIVIA DE FIERRO,

Lista de los trabajos de graduación correspondiente a los años 1955–1957. Papamá 1958. pp.[ii].vii. 73. [350.]*

CARMEN D. DE HERRERA, Lista bibliográfica de los trabajos de graduación y tesis presentados en la universidad 1939–1960. Universidad nacional: Panamá 1960. ff.iii.186. [1250.]*

BIBLIOGRAFÍA sobra la universidad de Panamá. Escuela de temporada: Biblioteca: [Panamá 1963]. ff.[i].42. [300.]

Panjab, university of the.

[MUHAMMAD AZAM SIDDIQI], Bibliography of theses, dissertations & research reports, university of the Panjab. West Pakistan bureau of education: Bibilographical [*sic*] series (no.ii): Lahore 1961. pp.[iii].v.212. [2086.]

Paris, university of.

CHARLES [MARIE GABRIEL BRÉCHILLET] JOURDAIN, Index chronologicus chartarum pertinentium ad historiam Universitatis parisiensis ab ejus originibus ad finam decimi sexti sæculi. Parisiis 1862. pp.[v].viii.433. [2197.]

E[UGÈNE PIERRE] ESTANAVE, Revue décennale des thèses présentées à la Faculté des sciences de Paris en vue du grade de docteur ès sciences, du 1er janvier 1891 au 31 décembre 1900, avec l'indication des périodiques contenant la plupart de ces mémoires ou leurs analyses. Arcis-sur-Aube 1901. pp.115. [347.]

NOÉ LEGRAND, La collection des thèses de l'ancienne Faculté de médecine de Paris depuis 1539 et son catalogue inédit jusqu'en 1793. Bibliothèque historique de la 'France médicale' (vol.l): 1913. pp.216. [1500.]

the theses listed cover the period 1763–1793 only.

TABLES (la première des noms des auteurs et la seconde des matières) des thèses soutenues à la Faculté de médecine de Paris. 1920 &c.

details of this work are entered under Academies: Medicine, above.

RÉPERTOIRE des thèses de droit comparé soutenues à la Faculté de droit de Paris pendant les années 1900 à 1930. Université de Paris: Faculté de droit: Bulletin de documentation législative et sociale (no.23): [1931]. pp.70. [1200.]

P. GLORIEUX, Répertoire des maîtres en théologie de Paris au XIIIe siècle. [Études de philosophie médiévale (vols.xvii–xviii):] 1933[–1934]. pp.[iii]. 468+[iii].518. [3500.]

ALBERT GUIGUE, La faculté des lettres de l'université de Paris depuis sa fondation (17 mars 1808), jusqu'au 1er janvier 1935. 1935. pp.[iv].373. [2000.] *consists in major part of lists of theses.*

GABRIEL GARNIER and ODETTE BARTHÉLEMY, Catalogue des thèses soutenues devant la Faculté de pharmacie de Paris de 1895 à 1940. 1941. pp.96. [802.]

— — Deuxième édition . . . augmentée des thèses soutenues de 1941 à 1959, par Suzanne Lavaud. 1960. pp.210. [1164.]

SUZANNE LAVAUD, Catalogue des thèses de doctorat ès sciences naturelles soutenues à Paris de 1891 à 1954. Faculté de pharmacie: Bibliothèque: Paris 1955. pp.257. [1181.]

Pennsylvania, university of.

BIBLIOGRAPHY of publications by [of] members of the faculty. University of Pennsylvania: Philadelphia.

    1938–1939. pp.44. [800.]
    1939–1940. pp.63. [1200.]
    1940–1941. pp.59. [1150.]
    1941–1942. pp.55. [1100.]

1942–1943. pp.64. [1200.]
1943–1944. pp.43. [800.]
1945. pp.46. [750.]
1946. pp.55. [800.]
1947. pp.70. [1000.]
1948. pp.80. [1100.]
1949. pp.88. [1125.]
1950. pp.119. [2000.]
1951. pp.61. [900.]

[*continued as:*]

Bibliography of faculty publications.

1952. pp.44. [750.]
1953. pp.51. [1500.]
1954. pp.54. [1500.]
1955. pp.53. [1500.]
1956. pp.61. [2000.]
1957. pp.70. [2000.]
1958. pp.71. [2000.]
1959. pp.84. [2000.]

no more published.

Pennsylvania state university.

PUBLICATIONS and research [and other contribu-tions]. Pennsylvania state college [university]: State College, Pa.

1930–1931. pp.11. [175.]
1931–1932. pp.15. [200.]
1932–1933. pp.16. [200.]
1933–1934. pp.
1934–1935. pp.42. [400.]
1935–1936. pp.54. [500.]
1936–1937. pp.59. [500.]
1937–1938. pp.57. [500.]
1938–1939. pp.
1939–1940. pp.62. [600.]
1940–1941. pp.62. [600.]
1941–1942. pp.61. [600.]
1942–1943. pp.64. [550.]
1943–1944. pp.53. [500.]
1944–1945. pp.76. [600.]
1945–1946. pp.67. [500.]
1946–1947. pp.85. [700.]
1947–1948. pp.119. [900.]
1948–1949. pp.136. [1000.]
1949–1950. pp.156. [1200.]
1950–1951. pp.149. [1200.]
1951–1952. pp.86. [1200.]
1952–1953. pp.93. [1200.]
1953–1954. pp.
1954–1955. pp.99. [1500.]
1955–1956. pp.105. [1500.]
1956–1957. pp.112. [1500.]

1957–1958. pp.108. [1500.]
1958–1959.
1959–1960. pp.129. [1700.]
1960–1961. pp.112. [1600.]
1961–1962. pp.
in progress.

BEVERLY RUFFIN, Graduate theses and disserta-
tions, 1892–1937. Pennsylvania state college:
Library studies (no.1 = Bulletin, vol.xxxii, no.1):
State College 1938. pp.[ii].ii.182. [2093.]

Peshawar, university of.

[MUSSAWIR ALI HAMIDI], Bibliography of theses,
dissertations & research reports, university of
Peshawar. West Pakistan bureau of education:

Bibliographical series (no.iii): Lahore [1961].
ff.[ii].6. [15.]*

Philippines, university of the.

THESES abstracts. University of the Philippines:
Graduate school of arts and sciences: [Quezon
City].
i. 1947–1954. 1962. pp.ix.118. [100.]
in progress.

Pittsburgh, university of.

[CHESTER ARTHUR BUCKNER], Annotations of theses and dissertations in education, university of Pittsburgh, School of education. Phi delta kappa: Xi chapter: Pittsburgh 1934. pp.[viii].56.

— [third edition]. Directory of holders of graduate degrees in education, with titles of theses and dissertations, university of Pittsburgh, School of education. [By John Alfred Nietz]. Phi delta kappa: Xi chapter: [Pittsburgh] 1945. pp.90. [3028.]

Princeton university.

LIST of references on Princeton university. Library of Congress: Washington 1915. ff.6. [88.]*

BIBLIOGRAPHY of faculty publications. Princeton university: Official register (vol.xxxiv, no.5a &c.): Princeton.

    1941–1942. . . . (vol.xxxiv, no.5a). pp.45. [400.]
    1942–1943. . . . (vol.xxxv, no.5). pp.77. [400.]
    1944–1946. . . . (vol.xxxviii, no.10). pp.74. [750.]

[*continued as:*]
A bibliography of Princeton faculty publications. Princeton university conference.★

    1954–1956. pp.iii–xv.127. [1000.]
    1956–1957. pp.[ix].62. [800.]
    1957–1958. pp.[ix].53. [800.]
    1958–1959. pp.[ix].57. [800.]
    1959–1960. pp.[ix].63. [800.]
    1960–1961. pp.[ix].71. [1000.]
    1961–1962. Edited by Jay K. Lucker. pp.xi.77.
    [1000.]
in progress.

Purdue university.

ESTHER M[ARTIA] SCHLUNDT, Guide to dissertations submitted in partial fulfillment of the requirements for the degree of doctor of philosophy at Purdue university. Lafayette, Ind.★

    1893–1949. 1956. pp.[v].116. [609.]
    1950–1953. 1958. pp.[v].83. [628.]

Radcliffe college.

SUMMARIES of theses accepted in partial fulfilment of the requirements for the degree of doctor of philosophy. Radcliffe college: Graduate school of arts and sciences: Cambridge [Mass.].

    1931–1934. pp.viii.166. [47.]

1935–1938. pp.viii.195. [50.]
in progress?

DOCTORS of philosophy, 1939–1945, with the titles of their theses. [Cambridge 1945]. pp.8. [100.]

Reading, university of.

CHRONOLOGICAL list of departmental publications. University of Reading: Agricultural economics department: [Reading] 1937 [&c.].
details of this work are entered under Agriculture: Agricultural economics, above.

ABSTRACTS of theses approved for the degrees of ph. d., m. a., and m. sc. in the university of Reading during the academic year.
    1957–1958. pp.vii.74. [34.]
    1958–1959. pp.vii.64. [39.]
    1959–1960. pp.vii.66. [37.]
    1960–1961. pp.vii.50. [31.]
    1961–1962. pp.vii.67. [41.]
    1962–1963. pp.vii.65. [41.]
in progress.

Rochester, university of.

CHECK list of masters' and doctors' theses accepted by the university of Rochester. [Rochester.]*

    [i]. 1897–1933. pp.[ii].36. [400.]
    ii. 1934–1938. pp.[ii].iv.41. [450.]
    iii. 1938–1943. pp.[ii].53. [550.]
    iv. 1943–1948. pp.ii.49. [500.]
    v. 1949–1953. pp.[v].78. [700.]
    vi. 1954–1958. pp.[v].75. [600.]
in progress.

Rostov, university of.

основные печатные работы сотрудников
РГУ. (Библиографический указатель).

    1959. pp.64. [607.]
    1960. pp.64. [642.]
in progress.

St Andrews, city and university of.

J[AMES] H[OUSTON] BAXTER, Collections towards a bibliography of St. Andrews. University
of St. Andrews: Library publications (vol.i): St.
Andrews 1926. pp.[ix].143. [1208.]

St John's university.

ABSTRACTS of dissertations. Brooklyn 1939 &c.
in progress.

St Louis university.

PUBLICATIONS and research in progress of faculty
members and students. Saint Louis university:
Bulletin (vol.xlix, no.14 &c.): St Louis.

    1952–1953. . . . (vol.xlix, no.14). pp.133.
    [1500.]
    1954–1955. . . . (vol.li, no.14). pp.128. [1500.]
    1955–1956. . . . (vol.52, no.13). pp.132.
    [1500.]
    1957–1958. . . . (vol.54, no.11). pp.153.
    [1750.]
in progress.

Salamanca, university of.

FRANZ EHRLE, Los manuscritos vaticanos de los
teologos salmantinos del siglo XVI. . . . Primera
edición española corregida y aumentada a carga
del padre José M. March. Biblioteca de 'Estudios
ecclesiásticas': Serie de opúsculos (vol.i): Madrid
1930. pp.xvi.136. [75.]

Salzburg, university of.

JUDAS THADDÄUS ZAUNER, Biographische nachrichten von den salzburgischen rechtslehrern von
der stiftung der universität an bis auf gegenwärtige
zeiten. Salzburg 1789. pp.[xvi].144. [500.]

San Carlos de Guatemala, universidad de.

GONZALO DARDON CÓRDOVA, Monografía bibliográfica de libros, folletos, separatas y artículos en revistas escritos por los catedráticos de la Facultad de humanidades de la universidad de San Carlos de Guatemala. Guatemala 1954. pp.38. [500.]

San Diego state college.

SAN DIEGO state college master of arts and master of science theses and projects 1950–1957. San Diego 1959. ff.[ii].86. [800.]*

San Marcos, universidad nacional mayor de.

CATÁLOGO de tesis de la Facultad de derecho. Universidad nacional mayor de San Marcos: [Lima] 1944. pp.149. [1000.]

Santo Tomas, universidad pontificia de.

INDICE de las obras publicadas por profesores de la universidad de Santo Tomas de Manila, Filipinas. Manila 1956. pp.89. [1500.]
also issued in an english edition.

São Paulo, university of.

CATÁLOGO das publicações periódicas da universidade de São Paulo. Universidade de São Paulo: Reitoria: Biblioteca central: São Paulo 1951. pp.[vi].52. [150.]

INDICE bibliográfico das publicações da universidade São Paulo. Institutos universitarios. Reitoria da universidade: Biblioteca central: São Paulo.

    i. Faculdade de direito. 1951. pp.112. [292.]

    ii. Escola politécnica. 1953. pp.157. [1601.]

    iii.

    iv. Faculdade de filosofia, ciências e letras. 1953. pp.75. [529.]

    v.

    vi.

    vii.

    viii. Faculdade higiene e saúde pública. 1953. pp.42. [138.]

    ix. Faculdade de ciências económicas e administrativas. 1951. pp.46. [181.]

no more published?

CATÁLOGO das publicações periódicas das instituições anexas e complementares da universidade de São Paulo. Universidade de São Paulo: Reitoria: Biblioteca central: 1953. pp.[iv].74. [70.]

Saragossa, university of.

MANUEL JIMÉNEZ CATALÁN, Memorias para la historia de la Universidad literaria de Zaragoza. Reseña bio–bibliográfica de todos sus grados mayores en las cinco [*sic*] facultades, desde 1583 a 1845. Zaragoza 1925 [*on cover:* 1926]. pp.584. [1000.]

Saratov, university of.

YU[LIYA] O[SIPOVNA] BIBILO and T. S. PENZINA, Труды научных работников Саратовского государственного университета имени Н. Г. Чрнышевского. Библиографический указатель. Саратовский... университет: Научная библиотека: [Саратов] 1959. pp.238. [3965.]

Sheffield, university of.

SUMMARIES of theses submitted by successful candidates for higher degrees. University of Sheffield.

1938–1939. pp.4. [6.]

Sind, university of.

BIBLIOGRAPHY of theses, dissertations & research reports, university of Sind. West Pakistan bureau of education: Bibliographical series (no.iv): Lahore [1961]. ff.[ii].10. [75.]★

Sofia, university of.

КАТАЛОГЪ на университетскитѣ издания. София.

> 1904–1942. Съставилъ Асенъ Ст. Кова-чевъ. 1943. pp.92. [3000.]

> 1943–1946. Съставил А. Ковачев. 1947. pp.31. [1000.]

ASEN ST. KOVACHEV, Библиография на Со-фийския университетъ "Св. Климентъ Ох-ридски", 1904–1942. Университетска биб-лиотека (no.263): София 1943. pp.vii.367. [3000.]

YU. VASILEVA, Библиография на изданиата на Софийския университет 1947–1955. София 1956. pp.108. [762.]

South Africa, university of.

A[NNA] M[ARIETA] DU PREEZ, Lys van verhande-lings en proefskrifte aanvaar deur die universiteit van Suid-Afrika, 1919–1958. Universiteit van

Suid-Afrika: Mededelings (no. C.8): Pretoria 1958. pp.96. [1200.]

SUMMARIES of theses accepted by the university of South Africa. University of South Africa: Communications (no.C19 &c.): Pretoria.

> 1959. C. F. J. Muller, ed. . . . (no.C19). pp.50. [20.]
>
> 1960. J. L. Steyn, ed. . . . (no.C25). pp.62. [20.]

Southampton, university of.

ABSTRACTS of theses accepted for higher degrees in the university of Southampton. [Southampton].

> 1955–1956. pp.21. [17.]
> 1956–1957.
> 1957–1958. pp.32. [27.]
> 1958–1959. pp.27. [21.]
> 1959–1960. pp.44. [32.]
> 1960–1961. pp.40. [31.]
> 1961–1962. pp.56. [45.]
> 1962–1963. pp.64. [52.]
> *in progress.*

Southern California, university of.

EMORY S[TEPHEN] BOGARDUS, *ed.* Trends in scholarship. Annotations of theses and dissertations accepted by the university of Southern California, 1910–1935. University of Southern California: Publications: University chronicles series (no.4): Los Angeles 1936. pp.181.133. [4008.]

FREDERICK J. WEERSING, *ed.* Annotated index of theses and dissertations. University of Southern California: School of education: Alpha epsilon chapter of Phi delta kappa: [Los Angeles] 1936. pp.[vi].133.

GERALD J. GIEFER, LOIS JUDD and CYNTHIA BARNES, Theses on water resources, Stanford university, California institute of technology and university of Southern California. University of California: Report (no.7): Berkeley 1959. pp.iv.81. [561.]*

Southern university.

PUBLICATIONS of the faculty, 1950–1960. Southern university and agricultural and mechanical college [Scottlandville]: Bulletin (vol.xlvi, no.3): Baton Rouge [1960]. pp.32. [400.]*

Sredneaziatsky gosudarstvennuy universitet.

УКАЗАТЕЛЬ изданий Средне-азиатскаго государственного университета. 1.[1922–1929]. Ташкент 1930. pp.[iv].31. [112.]

o. v. maslova, Систематический указатель к изданиям... с 1922–1950 гг. Средне-азиатский государственный университет: Материалы к библиографии (vol.ii): Ташкент 1952. pp.119. [1500.]

— — Издание 2-е. И Составители... О. В. Маслова, В. А. Вяткина, А. И. Корми-лицин .... (vol.viii): 1958. pp.192. [2026.]

Stanford university.

list of publications by members of the depart-ment of geology of the Leland Stanford junior university. [Palo Alto] 1903. pp.25. [250.]

alice n. hays, *ed.* University bibliography for the academic year September 1, 1938 to August 31, 1939. Stanford 1939. pp.v.67. [1200.]

earlier and later issues form part of the Annual report of the president of the university.

publications of the faculty. Stanford univer-sity: [Stanford].*

    1948–1949. ff.[i].58. [750.]
    1949–1950. ff.[i].68. [1000.]
    1950–1951. ff.[i].64. [900.]
    1951–1952. ff.[i].69. [1000.]

1952–1953. ff.[iii].62. [900.]
1953–1954. ff.[iii].78. [1200.]
1954–1955. ff.[iii].79. [1200.]
1955–1956. ff.[iii].76. [1200.]
1956–1957. ff.[iii].77. [1200.]
1957–1958. ff.[iii].88. [1300.]
1958–1959. ff.[iii].107. [1600.]
1959–1960. ff.[iii].114. [1700.]
1960–1961. ff.[iii].102. [1500.]

in progress.

GERALD J. GIEFER, LOIS JUDD and CYNTHIA BARNES, Theses on water resources, Stanford university, California institute of technology and university of Southern California. University of California: Water resources center archives: Report (no.7): Berkeley 1959. pp.iv.81. [561.]*

Strasbourg, university of.

VERZEICHNISS der an der Kaiser-Wilhelms-universität Strassburg vom sommer-semester

1872 bis ende 1884 erschienenen schriften. Strassburg 1890. pp.[ii].74.

[OSCAR BERGER-LEVRAULT], Catalogue analytique et bibliographique des thèses soutenues devant les académies et universités successives de

Strasbourg. [1891]. pp.46. [100.]

LES PUBLICATIONS de la Faculté des lettres de Strasbourg. Université de Strasbourg: [Strasbourg] 1936. pp.88. [100.]

Suomen teknillinen korkeakoulu.

LIST of dissertations for the degree of doctor of technology, 1911–1953. Helsinki 1953. ff.19. [100.]*
reproduced on yellow paper from typewriting.

Swansea, university of.

UNIVERSITY departments of geography higher degree theses. [Swansea].*
> 1956–1960. [By William George Victor Balchin]. pp.9. [200.]
> 1960–1961. pp.12. [300.]
in progress.

Sydney, university of.

[JOHN LE GAY BRERETON], Bibliographical record of the university of Sydney, 1851–1913. Sydney 1914. pp.96. [1750.]

RESEARCH and scholarship in the university ot
Sydney. Sydney.

  1954.

  1955.

  1956. pp.153. [500.]

  1957.

  1958. pp.165. [500.]

Syracuse university.

LIST of publications. Syracuse university: New
York state college of forestry: [Syracuse] 1929.
pp.10. [200.]

— [another edition]. Publications. 1960. pp.12.
[200.]*

FACULTY publications and creative work.
[Syracuse].*

  1957–1958. ff.64. [750.]

  in progress?

Szeged university.

ISTVANNÉ BEZERÉDI, PÁL BÓDAY and AURÉL
HENCZ, A Szegedi tudományegyetem dolgo-
zóinak 1954. évi szakirodalmi munkássága.
Bibliográfia. Acta universitatis szegediensis: Acta
bibliothecaria (vol.i): Szeged 1955. pp.vi.70.
[415.]

  the university's medical publications are excluded

Special Subjects

Tartu university.

TARTU riiklik ülikool. Ilmunud tööde bibliografia. Tartu 1960 &c.
in progress.

LEO TIIK, Tartu riiklikus ülikoolis 1946–1959 kaitstud väitekirjad. Bibliograafia. Tartu 1961. pp.52. [228.]

Tasmania, university of.

RESEARCH report for 1960. [Hobart] [1962]. pp. [ii].ix.85. [300.]*

Temple university.

MAURICE F[ALCOLM] TAUBER, Index of theses and dissertations prepared at Temple university, 1908–1935. Philadelphia 1935. ff.[iii].44. [549.]*

J. PERIAM DANTON and MAURICE F[ALCOLM] TAUBER, Graduate theses and dissertations, 1894–1940. Temple university: Sullivan memorial library studies: Philadelphia 1940. pp.viii.93. [961.]

GRADUATE theses and dissertations, 1941–1950. Temple university: Library: Philadelphia 1953. pp.vi.48. [460.]

Tennessee, university of.

PUBLICATIONS of the faculty and staff of the university of Tennessee. University of Tennessee: Record (vol.65, no.3 &c.): Knoxville.

1957–1958.... (vol.65, no.3): 1962. pp.[v].54. [1000.]

1959. Compiled by Kenneth Curry. . . . (vol.63, no.4): 1960. pp.[v].62. [750.]

1960.... (vol.64, no.4): 1961. pp.[v].72. [900.]

1961. . . . (vol.66, no.1): 1963. pp.[v].81. [1000.]

1962. . . . (vol.66, no.3): 1963. pp.[v].82. [1000.]

in progress.

Texas, university of.

[CHARLES CURTIS CUMBERLAND], Classified list of master of arts dissertations in history, 1895–1940 inclusive. University of Texas: [Austin 1941]. ff.[i].iii.63. [1000.]★

DOCTORAL degrees conferred, the Graduate school, the university of Texas, 1915–1943. University of Texas: Publication (no.4417): Austin 1944. pp.44.

PUBLICATIONS by members of the faculty of the university of Texas. Austin.

1945. pp.[ii].59. [600.]
1946–1947. pp.[v].149. [750.]*
1948–1954. pp.viii.360. [6000.]
1955–1956. pp.ix.260. [3000.]
1957–1958. pp.viii.312. [5000.]
1959–1960. 1963. pp.ix.414. [6000.]

in progress.

WILLIAM R. SHUNK and FRANKLIN PARKER, History of education, philosophy of education and comparative education: annotated bibliography of doctoral dissertations at the university of Texas 1923–1958. University of Texas: Department of history and philosophy of education: [Austin] 1959. ff.[66]. [81.]*

Texas christian university.

BIBLIOGRAPHY of theses accepted by Texas christian university and Brite college of the Bible, 1909–1954. Texas christian university: Bulletin (vol.53, no.4): [Fort Worth 1957]. pp.iv.37. [604.]

Special Subjects

Texas technological college.

JOE B[ILL] LEE, Bibliography of theses accepted by the Texas college of arts and industries, 1936–1958. Kingsville 1958. ff.iii.37. [526.]★

THESES accepted by Texas technological college. Texas technological college: Library: Library bulletin (no.1 &c.): [Lubbock].

–1950. Compiled by Sarah E. Taylor. . . . (no.1): 1951. pp.51. [900.]

1951–1955. . . . (no.4): 1956. pp.63. [300.]

1956–1960. Compiled by Sibyl Anne Morrison. . . . (no.6): 1961. pp.90. [400.]

Toulouse, university of.

LISTE des thèses de doctorat en médecine et pharmacie soutenues devant la faculté mixte de médecine et pharmacie de l'université de Toulouse.

1936–1937. pp.10. [140.]

1937–1938. pp.8. [100.]

RAPPORT annuel du conseil de l'université. Comptes rendus des travaux des facultés, des instituts et des observatoires.

1944–1945. 1947. pp.123. [500.]

1945–1946. 1949. pp.215. [500.]
1946–1947. 1949. pp.175. [500.]
1947–1948. 1950. pp.156. [500.]
1949–1956.
1957–1958. 1961. pp.332. [1000.]
1958–1959. 1962. pp.347. [1000.]
1959–1960. 1963. pp.391. [1500.]
in progress.

Tübingen, university of.

CHRISTIAN FRIEDRICH SCHNURRER, Biographische und litterarische nachrichten von ehemaligen lehrern der hebräischen litteratur in Tübingen. Ulm 1792. pp.vi.274. [250.]

Tulane university.

TITLES of theses, 1885–1937. New Orleans 1939. pp.31. [635.]

FACULTY research and publications. [New Orleans.]
[i]. 1939–1941. pp.68. [1000.]
[ii]. 1946–1948. pp.70. [1000.]
[iii]. 1948–1950. pp.66. [1000.]
iv. 1950–1952. pp.84. [1500.]
v. 1952–1954. pp.72. [1250.]

not published for 1941–1946; merged with Abstracts of dissertations and theses *and continued as:*

Faculty publications and lists of dissertations and theses.

1954–1956. pp.55. [800.]

Turku, university of.

ANDREAS ANTONIUS STJERNEMAN [ANDERS ANTON STIERNMAN], Aboa literata, continens omnes fere scriptores qui aliquid ab academiae ejusdem incunabulis a.C. 1640 in lucem publicam edidisse pro tempore deprehenduntur. Holmiae 1719. pp.[9].172. [700.]

the Bibliothèque nationale copy contains manuscript notes.

ELLI KIVIRANTA, Turun yliopiston julkaisema kirjallisuus vv. 1917–1946. Turun yliopiston kirjaston julkaisuja (no.3): Turku 1948. pp.32. [500.]

J[ORMA VÄINÖ] VALLINKOSKI, Turun akatemian väitöskirjat 1642–1828. Helsingin yliopiston kirjaston julkaisuja (no.30): Helsinki 1962– . pp. 128+

in progress.

Universitatea regele Ferdinand I.

I[OACHIM] CRĂCIUN, Activitatea ştiinţifica la

Special Subjects

Universitatea regele Ferdinand 1 din Cluj . . .
1920–1930. Bibliotheca bibliologica (vol.iii): Cluj
1935 [*on cover:* 1936]. pp.321. [5129.]

Upsala, university of.

J[OHAN] VON BAHR and [GUSTAF] TH[EODOR]
BRANDBERG, Upsala universitets matrikel. Upsala
1896. pp.viii.183. [2000.]

AKSEL ANDERSSON, Upsala universitets styres-
män, lärare och tjänstemän, 1872–1897. Schema-
tisk öfversikt och bio-bibliografi. Upsala 1897.
pp.185. [6000.]
also issued as the third volume of Upsala universitet 1872–1897. Festskrift, *1897.*

ERNST [LUDVIG PHILIP] MEYER, Program utgifna
vid Upsala universitet 1599–1700. Bibliografi.
[Uppsala universitets årsskrift:] Upsala 1905. pp.
162. [1163.]
— — 1701–1854. 1908. pp.[iii].132.vi. [885.]

ÅKE DINTLER and J[OHN] C[ARL] SUNE LINDQVIST,
Uppsala universitets matrikel, 1937–1950. Uppsala
1953. pp.628. [15,000.]

UPPSALA universitets bibliografi för det akademiska året. Uppsala.

1956–1957. pp.15–64. [1200.]
1957–1958. pp.16–83. [1300.]
1958–1959. pp.12–71. [1300.]

SCRIPTA academica. Écrits académiques et thèses de l'université d'Uppsala. Uppsala 1957 &c.
in progress.

Utah, university of.

[HECTOR LEE], A bibliography of the archives of the Utah humanities research foundation, 1944–1947. University of Utah: Bulletin (vol.38, no.9): Salt Lake City 1947. pp.[ii].41. [400.]

JANET C. DAVEY, Abstracts of doctoral dissertations 1947–1956 for degrees awarded at the university of Utah. University of Utah: Bulletin (vol.50, no.15): Salt Lake City 1959. pp.250. [400.]

INDEX of publications of the Bureau of economic and business research, university of Utah. [Salt Lake City] 1961. ff.[ix].36. [400.]*

Utrecht, university of.

FRANS KETNER, Album promotorum quo inde ab anno MDCXXXVI° usque ad annum MDCCCV^{nm} in Academia rheno-trajectina gradum doctoratus adepti sunt. Utrecht 1936. pp.278. [5000.]

G[ERRIT] A[LBERT] EVERS [*and others*], Lijst van gedrukte geschriften over de rijksuniversiteit te Utrecht. Proeve eener bibliographie, 1634–1936. Utrecht 1937. pp.viii.245. [3500.]
—— Aanvulling.
   1634–1936. pp.viii.76. [1500.]
   1941–1951. pp.viii.73. [1300.]

Valencia, university of.

ABELARDO PALANCA PONS, Guía bibliográfica de la universidad de Valencia. Junta técnica de archivos, bibliotecas y museos: Ediciones conmemorativas del centenario del Cuerpo facultativo (vol.ii): Madrid 1958. pp.3–271. [1400.]

Valladolid, university of.

HISTORIA de la universidad de Valladolid. Anales universitarios (vol.iii &c.): Valladolid.

   Expedientes de provisiones de cátedras . . . por Mariano Alcocer Martínez . . . (vol.iii): [1921]. pp.xv.445. [2000.]
   Hacienda universitaria y jurisdicción del rector. Por M. Alcocer Martínez . . .

(vol.iv): [1922]. pp.xl.296. [5000.]

Bio-bibliografías de juristas notables. Por M. Alcocer [y Martínez] y Saturnino Rivera [Manescau] ... [vol.v]: 1924 [1925]. pp.190. [250.]

Bio-bibliografías de teólogos notables. Por ... M. Alcocer y Martínez ... [vol.vi]: 1930. pp.xxxii.450.lxv. [1000.]

Bio-bibliografías de médicos notables. Por ... M. Alcocer y Martínez ... [vol.vii]: 1931. pp.xxi[*sic*, xiii].466.xxxii. [1500.]

Vanderbilt university.

ABSTRACTS of theses. Vanderbilt university: Bulletin (vol.xxxii, no.9 &c.): Nashville, Tenn.

1931–1932 ... (vol.xxxii, no.9): 1932. pp.84. [70.]

1932–1933 ... (vol.xxxiii, no.9): 1933. pp.74. [60.]

1933–1934 ... (vol.xxxiv, no.9): 1934. pp.64. [50.]

1934–1935 ... (vol.xxxv, no.9): 1935. pp.48. [40.]

1935–1936 ... (vol.xxxvi, no.10): 1936. pp.69. [50.]

1936–1937 ... (vol.xxxvii, no.9): 1937. pp.81.

[70.]
1937–1938 . . . (vol.xxxviii, no.11): 1938.
pp.67. [50.]
1938–1939 . . . (vol.xxxix, no.10): 1939.
pp.79. [70.]

PUBLICATIONS of the faculty members . . . 1930
. . . 1935. Vanderbilt university: Bulletin (vol.
xxxvi, no.9): Nashville, Tenn. pp.32. [400.]

Venezuela, universidad central de.

NÓMINA de las publicaciones periódicas de
distribución general. Caracas 1961. ff.[i].4. [19.]*

Vienna, university of.

VERZEICHNIS über die seit dem jahre 1872 an der
philosophischen fakultät der universität in Wien
eingereichten und approbierten dissertationen.
Universität: Wien 1935–1936. pp.[iii].283+[iii].
298+[iii].434. [9171.]
— Verzeichnis der 1934 bis 1937 an der philosophischen fakultät der universität in Wien und
der 1872 bis 1937 an der philosophischen fakultät
der universität in Innsbruck eingereichten [&c.].
1937.

GUSTAV GUGITZ, Bibliographie zur geschichte und stadtkunde von Wien. Verein für landeskunde von Niederösterreich und Wien: Wien 1947–1962. pp.[vii].504 + 265 + [iv].492 + 468 +360. [25,000.]

the author's name does not appear in the first volume.

LISL ALKER, Verzeichnis der an der universität Wien approbierten dissertationen, 1937–1949. Wien 1952–1954. pp.x.206+xi.104. [4496.]

WALTER STURMINGER, Bibliographie und ikonographie der Türkenbelagerungen Wiens 1529 und 1683. Kommission für neuere geschichte Österreichs: Veröffentlichungen (no.41): Graz&c. 1955. pp.xvi.420. [4270.]

Virginia, university of.

ABSTRACTS of dissertations accepted in partial fulfilment of the requirements for the degree of doctor of philosophy. University of Virginia: Department of graduate studies: Charlottesville.

    1931–1932. pp.12. [16.]
    1932–1933. pp.13–22. [13.]
    1933–1934. pp.23–25. [17.]
    1935. pp.64. [25.]
    1936. pp.[vii].128. [24.]

1937. pp.108. [22.]
1938. pp.119. [26.]
1939. pp.137. [27.]
1940. pp.141. [26.]
1941. pp.97. [21.]
1942. pp.83. [19.]
1943. pp.57. [20.]
1944. pp.76. [16.]
1945–1947. pp.227. [53.]
1948. pp.169. [30.]
1949. pp.150. [39.]
1950. pp.176. [36.]

no more published.

Virginia polytechnic institute.

RALPH MINTHORNE BROWN, V. P. I. historical index, October 1, 1872 to December 31, 1941. Virginia polytechnic institute: Bulletin (vol.xxxv, no.12): Blacksburg [1942]. pp.62. [1417.]

GRADUATE theses accepted by V. P. I. Virginia polytechnic institute: Bulletin (vol.xliv, no.6 &c.): Blacksburg.

[i]. 1892–1951. . . . (vol.xliv, no.6). pp.52. [1500.]
ii. 1951–1954.
iii. 1955–1957. . . . (vol.l, no.8). pp.20. [300.]
iv. 1958–1959. . . . (vol.lii, no.7). pp.20. [300.]

Virginia state college.

M[AMIE] W[HITE] CAMPBELL and J[AMES] A[LEX-ANDER] HULBERT, A bibliography of graduate masters theses written at Virginia state college, 1937–1949. Petersburg 1949. pp.29. [132.]

Wales, university of.

LIST of some of the works published by members of the teaching staffs of the constituent colleges and of the Welsh national school of medicine and by fellows and postgraduate students of the university in the academic year, 1931–1932. Prifysgol Cymru: Oswestry [printed] [1932]. pp.26. [300.]

HANDLIST of publications, 1924–1945. University college of Wales: Department of agricultural economics: Aberystwyth 1945. pp.[iv].33. [350.]*

Washington, university of, Seattle.

A LIST of university of Washington publications. University of Washington: Bulletin (no. 210): Seattle 1927. pp.30. [350.]

CLARA J. KELLY, Publications of the university of Washington faculty, November 4, 1861–March 31, 1936. University of Washington: Publications: Library series (no.1): Seattle 1937. pp.316. [4000.]

AKIKO A[RAI] CRAVEN, Theses and dissertations accepted ... for advanced degrees at the university of Washington, 1946/47–1955/56. [Seattle] 1959. pp.[488]. [3445.]*

Washington, university of, St Louis.

PUBLICATIONS of the members of the faculty of Washington university. Washington university: Studies (vol.xiii, Supplement): St. Louis 1925. pp.26. [400.]

covers the period 1923–1925; continued as:

University bibliography. Washington university: Studies (n.s.).

　　　1925–1926. pp.23. [300.]
　　　　　　[*continued as:*]

Faculty publications.

　　　1926–1927. pp.19. [250.]
　　　1928–1929. pp.30. [450.]
　　　　　　[*continued as:*]

Annual bibliography.

　　　1929–1930. pp.36. [500.]
　　　1930–1931. pp.29. [400.]
　　　1931–1932. pp.42. [600.]
　　　1932–1933. pp.34. [500.]
　　　1933–1934. pp.36. [500.]
　　　1934–1935. pp.36. [500.]

1935–1936. pp.41. [600.]
1936–1937. pp.41. [600.]
1937–1938. pp.42. [600.]
1938–1939. pp.45. [600.]
1939–1940. pp.49. [600.]
1940–1941. pp.50. [600.]
1941–1942. pp.48. [600.]
1942–1943. pp.48. [600.]
1943–1944. pp.40. [600.]
1944–1945. pp.48. [600.]
1945–1946. pp.51. [650.]
1946–1947. pp.59. [750.]
1947–1948. pp.70. [900.]
1948–1949. pp.74. [1000.]
1949–1950. pp.105. [1500.]
1950–1951. pp.105. [1500.]
in progress.

FACULTY research publications. Washington university: St. Louis.

1956–1957. pp.[ii].22. [350.]
in progress?

DOCTORAL dissertations and masters' theses accepted by Washington university. St. Louis.

1956–1957. pp.[ii].16. [108.]★
in progress?

DIRECTORY university investigations, research in

progress, faculty publications, dissertations and theses. St Louis, Mo. 1958. pp.[iii].75. [1500.]

Wayne university.

BIBLIOGRAPHY of master's theses, 1932–1940. Detroit 1941. pp.[16]. [400.]

Western reserve university.

BIBLIOGRAPHY of publications by members of the faculties, abstracts of dissertations by graduate students of Western reserve university. Cleveland.*

  1954–1956. pp.[v].416. [750.]
  1956–1958. pp.[v].420. [750.]
  in progress.

West Virginia state college.

PUBLICATIONS of the faculty and staff of West Virginia state college, January 1, 1946–December 31, 1959. West Virginia state college: Bulletin (ser.47, no.5): Institute 1959. pp.23. [450.]

West Virginia university.

GRADUATE research in education, West Virginia university, 1898–1959. Morgantown 1959. pp. [iii].139. [977.]*

Special Subjects

Wichita, municipal university of.

DISSERTATIONS accepted for higher degrees in the graduate school. Municipal university of Wichita: Bulletin (vol.x, no.12): [Wichita] 1935. pp.11. [125.]

Wilno university.

JACEK LIPSKI, Archiwum kuratorji Wileńskiej X. Ad. Czartoryskiego. Kraków 1926. pp.iii–xvi. 310. [very large number.]

Wisconsin, university of.

SUMMARIES of doctoral dissertations. Madison.
   i. 1935–1936. pp.[xx].350. [125.]
   ii. 1936–1937. pp.xxi.350. [125.]
   iii. 1937–1938. pp.[xxiii].372. [150.]
   iv. 1938–1939. pp.284. [150.]
   v. 1939–1940. pp.298. [150.]
   vi. 1940–1941. pp.354. [175.]
   vii. 1941–1942. pp.vi.360. [175.]
   viii. 1942–1943. pp.viii.240. [125.]
   ix. 1943–1947. pp.[viii].571. [250.]*
   x. 1947–1949. pp.[vi].694. [400.]*
   xi. 1949–1950. pp.[vi].439. [250.]*
   xii. 1950–1951. pp.[viii].540. [300.]*

xiii. 1951–1952. pp.viii.469. [275.]*
xiv. 1952–1953. pp.viii.530. [325.]*
xv. 1953–1954. pp.viii.711. [425.]*
xvi. 1954–1955. pp.viii.639. [400.]*

Wittenberg, university of.

FRIEDRICH BOERNER, Memoriae professorvm medicinae in Academia wittembergensi inde a primis illivs initiis renovatae specimen primum [–secvndvm]. Lipsiae [1755-1756]. pp.xx+xx. [200.]

JOHANN CHRISTOPH ERDMANN, Lebensbeschreibungen und litterarische nachrichten von den wittenbergschen theologen seit der stiftung der universität 1502. Wittenberg 1804. pp.[iii].220. [250.]

Yale university.

[IRVING FISHER], Bibliographies of the present officers of Yale university. New Haven [printed] 1893. pp.160. [4500.]

DOCTORS of philosophy of Yale university with the titles of their dissertations, 1861–1915. Graduate school: New Haven 1916. pp.210. [497.]

Zürich, university of.

[HEINRICH WEBER and JAKOB WERNER], Verzeichnis zürcherischer universitätsschriften, 1833–
1897. Im anhang: programmarbeiten der kantons-
schule Zürich, 1834–1903. Bibliothek der canto-
nal-lehranstalten: Katalog (vol.iv): Zürich 1904.
pp.vii.218. [1845.]

MAR 8 1972